DISCOVERING THE LEADER WITHIN

RUNNING SMALL GROUPS SUCCESSFULLY

RANDY FUJISHIN

West Valley College
Saratoga, California

ACADA BOOKS
San Francisco

Copyeditor: David Sweet
Proofreader: Andrea Goldman
Indexer: Patricia Deminna
Book and Cover Designer: Andrea DuFlon
Compositor: Pale Moon Productions

For information, please contact:
Acada Books, Inc.
1850 Union Street Suite 1216
San Francisco, California 94123

ISBN: 0-9655029-1-0
Library of Congress Catalog Card Number: 96-79626

Printed in the United States of America
10 9 8 7 6 5 4 3 2 1

CONTENTS

PREFACE

Working in groups is a part of your life. Whether you're the chair-person of a committee, a volunteer in a fund raising group, a member of an assembly team, or the head of a family reunion planning committee, you will be working with others in small groups to solve problems.

The purpose of this book is to provide you with a basic understanding of solving problems in a small group setting and the skills necessary to participate in and lead effective group discussion. I purposely kept citation of research to a minimum to facilitate reading and understanding, but provided a bibliography of pertinent books and articles for your further investigation.

Unlike other books dealing with group problem-solving, this book emphasizes your personal growth and development as you work with others in the group process. Furthermore, the knowledge and skills you gain from this book will enable you to discover the leader within you—that part of you that helps the group achieve its goals.

Chapter 1 examines the basic elements and characteristics of a problem-solving group and introduces you to a systems perspective for understanding group dynamics—the interconnectedness of member behavior.

In Chapter 2 you are encouraged to explore who you are apart from the group, and discover what's important and meaningful to you. Without this self-knowledge, your participation in group work can be easily sidetracked.

Chapters 3 and 4 present the fundamental skills necessary for speaking and listening in a group. I not only outline speaking and listening competencies for group discussion, but I also discuss their application to your personal life.

Chapter 5 explores decision-making techniques and the problem-solving agenda. This chapter focuses on effective methods for making decisions in groups, as well as a step-by-step process for solving problems.

Chapter 6 examines the preparation necessary for effective group discussion. We'll discuss where to look, what to look for, and how to organize your research. In addition to the preparation process, the chapter addresses the basic elements of critical thinking—testing evidence and reasoning.

Chapters 7 and 8 outline specific behaviors you can use to guide and lead the discussion process itself. These behaviors enable you to facilitate and lead the task and social dimensions of any group.

Chapter 9 discusses methods for building a cohesive and supportive group atmosphere and examines the importance of making group members feel successful, connected, valued, supported, and trusted.

Managing conflict is the topic of Chapter 10. It provides specific strategies for dealing with procedural, substantive, and interpersonal conflict within the group, as well as practical ways to use forgiveness to resolve small group conflicts.

After reading this book, you will be better equipped to participate more effectively in any problem-solving group. Not only will your communication skills and understanding of group process be enhanced, your willingness to facilitate and lead groups will be strengthened, for you will have discovered the leader within.

ACKNOWLEDGMENTS

I would like to thank Brian Romer for his belief in my original manuscript. His vision, wisdom, and passion as a publisher will always be appreciated. My deep gratitude goes to my editor, Robin Geller, whose skillful guidance and gentle reassurance brought my manuscript to a level worthy of publication. I am deeply indebted to Brian and Robin for the care and attention they gave in bringing this book to life.

Dr. Roberta A. Davilla, University of Northern Iowa; Dr. Joann Keyton, The University of Memphis; Dr. John Oetzel, Citrus College; Theodore E. Reavis, John F. Kennedy University; and Susan Welch, Mesa Community College provided valuable suggestions that helped make the book something I'm especially proud to share. I want to thank David Sweet for his expert copyediting of the manuscript. My deep appreciation goes to Paul D. Sanders for his encouragement, enthusiasm for life, and friendship. Van D. Cummings deserves special thanks for his interest and support of my writing projects. And I want to express my gratitude to my parents, Mike and Helen Fujishin, for the love they have given me all these years.

Finally, I would like to thank my wife, Vicky, whose love, goodness, and grace have shaped my life. She is my best friend, counselor, and source of joy. To Vicky, I dedicate this book.

ONE
WORKING IN A GROUP

**The real voyage of discovery consists not in seeking
new landscapes, but in having new eyes.
–Marcel Proust**

The best journeys in life provide us with a new way of seeing the world. Whether it's a month-long expedition to the Himalayas or a 30-minute visit with an old friend, we come away from these experiences with a greater understanding and appreciation of others and ourselves. We are not the same; we are changed. With new eyes, we see that we are capable of becoming more than we once believed. And with new eyes, we see that we can be freer, happier, and stronger than we once thought.

The best journeys in life, we discover, bring us closer to our truer selves.

One such journey took place for me in a cramped, cheerless conference room in Santa Barbara many years ago. I was a part-time employee at a small electronics company during my sophomore year of college, and I was asked to participate in a problem-solving group that would recommend ways to boost employee morale.

My previous experience with problem-solving groups was limited to a few semesters of high-school government and two group projects—one for an undergraduate psychology course and one for an English study group. All three experiences proved disastrous. The meetings were disorganized, adversarial, and long. Invariably one person would monopolize the discussion, while the rest of us would roll our eyes and watch the clock. We accomplished very little. And at the end of the meetings (which always ran longer than planned), we left the room feeling confused, frustrated, and often angry.

So when I arrived at our first meeting in that small, cluttered conference room in Santa Barbara, I was not expecting anything different. I was the youngest of the seven-member group. The other six were full-time employees in their 30s and 40s. And I felt inadequate and unnecessary. Before we sat down, the team leader introduced himself to me and offered me a soft drink. Once the meeting began, I was surprised by the organized flow of the discussion. The leader skillfully kept us on track, occasionally summarized the ideas that were being considered, and often complimented us for contributing other ideas. He even asked me for my thoughts a number of times as I sat silently watching the dance of the discussion.

Before I knew it, the leader was highlighting the main proposals we had generated, previewing the next step in the process, and thanking us for our work. That first meeting ended in less than one hour!

There were five more meetings after this initial session, and each one ran as smoothly as the first. We had our moments of disagreement and conflict during the six hours, but our team leader was skillful in guiding the discussion, accepting of our differences, and insightful in focusing and synthesizing our ideas.

In the end, I no longer regarded working in groups as something to be avoided. Rather, working in groups was something that could be productive, exciting, and even fun. Because of that experience, I literally saw a different world. And a different me.

WORKING IN GROUPS

Since that journey into the conference room, I have worked with a variety of problem-solving groups, both as a leader and as a participant. As a college instructor, corporate consultant and trainer, and clinical therapist for over 20 years, I have worked with hundreds of groups. Of course, not every group runs as smoothly as the one I just described. In fact, I believe that problem-solving in small groups can be one of the most challenging activities. But I am also convinced that you and I can learn skills and discover strengths within ourselves to make this process more effective and rewarding.

Working in groups is a part of life. Whether you're the vice-president of marketing, a member of a PTA group, or the head of the high-school reunion planning committee, you will be working with others in small groups to solve problems.

At first glance, this activity may seem easy. All we do is sit around a table, talk, and accomplish things. What could be easier? But rather than experiencing unselfish cooperation, responsible preparation, and open communication in our problem-solving efforts, we are often shocked by the lack of cooperation, the inadequacy of preparation, and the poor communication skills of group members. And if we are really honest, we would also have to admit to our own inabilities and lack of understanding of this complicated process called group problem-solving.

The purpose of this book is to provide you with a basic understanding of solving problems in a small group and the skills necessary to participate in and lead effective group discussions.

This chapter examines the four elements of a problem-solving group, the group as a system, the power of one, and the characteristics of groups. Let's start with the four elements of a problem-solving group.

FOUR ELEMENTS OF A PROBLEM-SOLVING GROUP

A *problem-solving group* is three or more people who share a common task, interact face-to-face, and influence one another. Let's consider each element of our definition of a problem-solving group.

Three or More People

The minimum number of individuals needed to constitute a small group is three people. Two people do not make a group because their interaction is that of a couple, or *dyad.* In a dyad, one person speaks, the other listens and responds, and then the original speaker considers what is being said. In this situation, no third individual witnesses the event, and thus does not influence the interaction by serving as an audience to it. A dyad normally encourages more self-disclosure, simply because no audience or third party is present.

Most groups have little control over the number of participants. The size of the group might be determined by group policy, management, available people, or the size of the meeting room. Group membership can range from three to 30 people or more.

I believe the ideal number of members in a small group is five to seven. In a group this size, each member is encouraged to speak without the imposition of a large number of individuals serving as an audience. Also, a group of five to seven provides more input than smaller groups, while maintaining a comfortable level of intimacy that larger groups often lack. In this book, we'll examine and discuss groups of five to seven people.

Sharing a Common Task

The second essential element of a problem-solving group is that the group shares a problem it feels is worth solving. Whether it's brainstorming ways to generate money, selecting a candidate for a committee, or planning a coworker's retirement dinner, there is an identified task or goal the group must accomplish. That task is the primary purpose for the existence of the group.

Interacting Face-to-Face

The third element of a problem-solving group is that group members interact face-to-face. This means they will be able to see one another's faces. Usually this meeting will occur in the same room with all members physically present.

But now with the advent of video technology, videoteleconferencing permits the group members to see and hear one another without their being physically present in the same room. Teleconferencing still satisfies our "face-to-face" criterion, although most of the nonverbal communication occurring in such interactions is lost. *Nonverbal communication* is all communication that is neither spoken nor written; it includes such variables as body language, clothing, punctuality, gestures, distancing or proxemics, facial expressions, use of time, and seating arrangements. Research has consistently reminded us that nonverbal communication—how an individual communicates without speaking or writing—has more impact on the receiver of a message than words themselves.

Ideally, the problem-solving group meets around a single table, thereby providing as much nonverbal information as possible. Being physically close to other human beings provides an immeasurable advantage as you interact and communicate. It's always better to be able to see the face and the body of the person you're interacting with, rather than hearing a tinny voice over a phone receiver, because without the nonverbal cues, much information about content and speaker can be lost.

Influencing One Another

This final element is fundamental to the definition of a problem-solving group. A group member does not exist and operate in a vacuum, isolated from the other members. Each member's statements and behavior affect every other group member in some way, be it small or great. A thoughtful compliment, a subtle criticism, a raised eyebrow, or a complaining moan can communicate a message of monumental proportions, and its effect can last a lifetime.

The reason people have gathered in groups to solve problems since the beginning of recorded history is that they benefit from the pooled skills, knowledge, resources, and experience provided by the group. The group, with its collective resources, usually stands a greater chance for survival and success.

An individual is also influenced and affected by the other group members. You can learn from their information and grow from their suggestions; be persuaded by their arguments and challenged by their proposals; be hurt by their remarks and healed by their praises. You can be deflated by others' bickering and inspired by their encouragement. Each member influences and is influenced by other group members, whether he or she acknowledges this fact or not.

THE SMALL GROUP AS A SYSTEM

A common illusion is that we think we are separate from the other members of the group. We often tend to see our individual needs, behaviors, responses, and communication as separate, unconnected to those of our group members. Most of our behavior and thinking are self-motivated, and we often lack awareness of the intricate and profound connections the group has established in its web of interactions.

There are two ways to look at group interactions. The first way sees each member as distinct and disconnected from any substantial and meaningful tie with the other people, like lone cowboys meeting on a hill to chat, then galloping off in different directions. In other words, I enter into the group being me, and I leave the group being me. Nothing has changed in me, except that I've spent some time with other people. This is one perspective of group interaction.

A second way of viewing group interaction is as a living organism. We are each a part of this living organism. You're the heart, I'm the lungs, and the other members serve their respective functions of the body. When something happens to one part, all the other parts feel the effects. This is the essence of the systems perspective of group interaction and is valuable in understanding and appreciating small group process.

A *system* is defined as a set of objects that interrelate with one another to form a whole. If one object in the system changes, the others change in response. The emphasis in a systems perspective is not on the individual members, but rather on the group as a whole. Any group of people working together to solve a problem meets this definition of a system.

Now we'll consider five characteristics of a system—interdependence, wholeness, mutual influence, adaptation, and equifinality.

Interdependence

The first characteristic of a system is *interdependence*. Each group member depends on all the other members in one way or another. An obvious example is the absence of four of the five members at a meeting. Even though you are present, their absence makes it impossible for you to participate in the meeting. Another example is a group member not researching or producing a critical piece of information the group needs in order to proceed. One member's behavior, or lack of behavior, prevents the entire group from progressing. In many ways, you are connected to and dependent upon the actions of the other group members.

Wholeness

From a systems perspective, the focus of attention in group work is on *wholeness*, or the entire group, rather than on a particular individual. Each member is important. But once individual members become interrelated and form a working group, they acquire a collective life. The whole becomes greater than the sum of its parts. The group can take on characteristics—productivity, creativity, and responsiveness—that may not be characteristic of individual members.

The individuals can often become energized by the collective whole. They can achieve more productivity than any member could realize alone. This is often referred to as *synergy*—the group product is usually superior to the best individual product. In other words, two heads are better than one.

Mutual Influence

The third characteristic of a system is *mutual influence*, which implies that cause and effect are interchangeable. Each action or behavior serves as both a response to a previous behavior and a stimulus for a future action. This characteristic of systems theory makes any attempt to assign blame for any problematic behavior pointless, because that behavior was in response to a previous behavior. An example of this would be the "nag/withdraw" syndrome. A wife withdraws because her husband nags. But the husband insists he nags because she withdraws. Oftentimes it is pointless to assign blame, to point the finger at who started this whole mess, because the behaviors are so intertwined. Rather than blame, the wife and the husband should explore ways to alter or modify the pattern of "nag/withdraw." The focus is on modifying behavior patterns instead of seeking to blame or punish.

Adaptation

The fourth characteristic of a system is *adaptation.* A system will seek to adapt to fit the demands of a changing environment. The group's flexibility to modify its procedures, rules, communication patterns, even its way of thinking and feeling, is indicative of its ability to survive and is required for its overall health. The problem-solving group must remain flexible and willing to change in order to cope with the changing environment (people, issues, and circumstances). Groups that are rigid, dogmatic, and unwilling to explore and discover new ways of operating are doomed to mediocrity and often failure. The flexible group is a healthy group.

Equifinality

Finally, the fifth characteristic of a system is *equifinality,* the ability to accomplish a goal in many ways and from many starting points. The group must accept the fact that there are many ways to accomplish a goal or task, not just one right way. We have been taught you can skin a cat only one way, but in reality you can accomplish this rather bizarre task, or any task for that matter, in numerous ways. The concept of equifinality opens up the possibility and potential for creative approaches to solving problems, which includes seeing the "problem" from a variety of viewpoints. Many roads lead to the "good life." The secret is discovering the one that feels right to you.

THE POWER OF ONE

The emphasis of a systems approach to studying small group problem-solving is on the group as a whole. Yet according to systems theory, a change in one object in the system changes all the other objects in the system. Every behavior has its effect on the group—regardless of whether the behavior is negative and counterproductive, or positive and productive. In other words, your behavior, be it negative or positive, influences the group's interaction and final product. The beauty of a systems perspective on group process is that you have the power to influence and determine the direction and outcome of the group.

CHARACTERISTICS OF GROUPS

Now that we've examined how a group can operate as a system, let's explore some of the fundamental characteristics of groups—group formation, task and social dimensions of groups, norms and conformity, and two perspectives on group development.

Group Formation

Whenever I see a band of Hells Angels roaring down the freeway, a cluster of Boy Scouts pitching tents at a campground, or a group of protesters picketing city hall, I am reminded why individuals join others to form groups—because each member receives something personally from his or her affiliation with the group.

People join groups for a variety of reasons. Many of these reasons are conscious; some, perhaps, are unconscious. Interpersonal attraction to group members is one reason for membership. Joining to help accomplish the goal of the group is another reason. Some people join a group because of its activities, while others unite with the group for identity. There are many other reasons for group affiliation, but we'll examine these four now.

Interpersonal attraction.   We join certain groups because we are attracted to the group members—not attraction in the sense of romance and love, but in terms of likeness and affinity. We often join groups because of similarity in beliefs, ethnicity, economic status, or age. People join religious, social activist, or flying-saucer clubs because of common beliefs. Others join groups such as the Japanese-American Citizenship League, NAACP, and Mexican-American Youth Association for their ethnic similarities. Membership in a country club, the Millionaires Club, or a homeless shelter can be motivated by economic likeness. Finally, age can be a factor , as seen in the American Association of Retired People or a preschool play group.

Attraction to the group goal. People often join groups because of the goal or objectives the group seeks to achieve. Groups such as a volunteer wilderness rescue team, a Little League fund-raising group, or a politician's election campaign provide opportunities for individuals to help advance a cause or accomplish a specific goal. Once the goal is achieved the group will often disband. But this isn't necessarily so. Examples of long-term groups are Mothers Against Drunk Drivers, Alcoholics Anonymous, and Greenpeace.

Attraction to the group activities. The third reason an individual might join a group is to participate in the activities. Groups such as a social dancing club, a fraternity or sorority, a weight-lifting group, and a bird-watching club provide opportunities for people to gather with others who enjoy similar activities.

Attraction for identity. Many people join groups to discover or strengthen their identity and purpose for living. We determine our self-identity to a great extent by the people with whom we associate. Birds of a feather often flock together. Many of the groups identified above—churches, social organizations, and even the Hells Angels—can provide a person with a strong sense of identity and purpose.

As you consider why people join groups, you might have noticed some groups satisfy more than one purpose. For example, a religious organization can provide interpersonal attraction, common goals, activities, and identity. This is true for the majority of groups people join—there is rarely only one reason for group affiliation.

Although many of the groups we have discussed are not necessarily problem-solving groups, they provide ample opportunities to make decisions and solve problems. Even a social dancing club will occasionally need to plan a fund-raiser, arrange a dance with other clubs, or decide what to do with a member who makes others uncomfortable with overt flirting.

Task and Social Dimensions of Groups

Once membership in a problem-solving group is established, it is important to realize that interaction within the group occurs in two areas or dimensions—the task dimension and the social dimension. Each dimension covers a different aspect and purpose of the group's interactions.

The task dimension. Each problem-solving group must attempt to solve a problem. This is the work or task of the group. All efforts to this end are considered the task dimension of a problem-solving group. Researching the problem, analyzing the problem, brainstorming solutions, discussing the strengths and weaknesses of the solutions, reaching consensus on the best solution, and implementing the solution are all elements of the group's task dimension.

The social dimension.   While the group is busy doing its work in the task dimension, the social dimension is occurring simultaneously. This dimension concerns the relationships between the group members, one to another, and to the group as a whole. The social dimension is not separate from the task dimension, but rather is intertwined within the task dimension. A change in one produces a change in the other. We don't really understand all the subtle relationships between the task and social dimensions, but we can be certain they do influence each other.

Norms and Conformity

In every problem-solving group, the behavior of all group members is determined and regulated to a great extent by the norms operating at the explicit and implicit levels. Conformity or adherence to these norms provides many benefits to the group. And challenging group norms can be an important task of the effective group member.

Norms.   *Norms* are the rules that regulate the behavior of group members. Norms hold the group together, making smooth, predictable interaction possible. Norms provide the basic building blocks of group interaction. Without norms of behavior, the group could easily be thrust into confusion, alienation, and even hostility. We need to understand two types of norms in problem-solving groups.

The first type is *implicit norms*, which are norms not announced verbally or in writing by the group. They are understood by group members, either consciously or unconsciously, but are not orally stated. Norms such as keeping quiet when others are speaking, being polite, sitting face-to-face with other members, and avoiding obscenities are examples of implicit rules or norms.

The second type is *explicit norms*, which are orally stated or written down as a code of conduct or expected group behavior. Many groups will establish formal rules of behavior that members are expected to follow. For example, military organizations, weight reduction groups, and religious sects might provide new group members with a list of expected behaviors, either verbally or in writing.

Conformity to norms.   *Conformity* is the adherence to group norms. Why do group members obey or adhere to the norms of the group? There are many reasons for this. First, conformity to norms makes our lives easier. Rather than always having to consider and decide from circumstance to circumstance when to talk, whom to face, and which hand to shake, norms prescribe these behaviors. Conformity to norms makes life orderly, predictable, and organized. Second, adherence to norms makes the interactions within the group more productive. Rather than spending time debating which behaviors are acceptable and which are unacceptable, the efforts of the group can be directed to the task dimension. Third, conformity to norms provides each member with a sense of belonging and acceptance. Whether it's a secret group handshake, a moose lodge hat, or a certain style of dress, norms of behavior can make us feel like one of the group.

Challenging a group norm.   When in doubt about an ambiguous or confusing group norm, a simple technique for *clarifying an implicit norm* is to simply raise the question to the group. For instance, let's assume that for the past three meetings, most group members, including the leader, arrived 10 to 15 minutes later than the agreed-upon meeting time, but you have been punctual to every meeting. You could bring the implicit norm (arriving late to meetings is acceptable) to the group for discussion. You might say, "I've noticed many group members arrive 10 to 15 minutes after our agreed upon meeting time. Is this the accepted norm of the group? I need to have clarification on this, because if it is the accepted norm, I too will arrive late."

Most group members are not used to having implicit norms brought to the explicit level of oral discussion. I've discovered many issues of substantive and interpersonal conflict can be resolved during the early stages of group development if the group puts the issue on the table for all to see and discuss. Don't be afraid to make the invisible visible.

It's also important for you and the group to *challenge any explicit norm* you feel is illegal, unethical, or harmful to group members or others. History is filled with examples of men and women who without question or challenge followed the rules or norms of a group that brought pain and suffering to others. Just as you can challenge an implicit norm, you can challenge an explicit norm before the group. This requires some courage, because you might be challenging the leadership and power structure of the group. But if you feel deep in your heart that a particular norm is harming others, you owe it to yourself and others to speak.

Four Phases of Group Development: Perspective I

Every problem-solving group changes during the course of its existence. It has a life all its own. No two groups are exactly the same. However, Aubrey Fisher in 1970 identified a four-phase sequence of group development. This four-phase model consists of periods of orientation, conflict, emergence, and reinforcement.

1. Orientation.   Most members of new groups spend their first meeting or two getting to know one another. Group members often feel a high-level of anxiety and uncertainty because they have little or no previous history with one another. The orientation phase is devoted to letting the group members "break the ice" and get acquainted. Humorous remarks, polite behavior, social chitchat, and conflict avoidance are characteristic of this group development phase. This phase is often referred to as *primary tension*—the uneasiness group members feel because they are unfamiliar with one another.

The social dimension of the group is overemphasized during this time because the establishment of a warm, supportive, and trusting environment is crucial to the group's task dimension in later phases of its development.

It is also during the orientation phase that members begin to initiate discussion about the task before them. Discussion about the nature and scope of the problem or task begins. Group members will often state their opinions and feelings in tentative, vague language, because they might not yet be comfortable fully disclosing their positions on issues.

2. Conflict.   After group members are comfortable enough to share their opinions and feelings at a deeper level, they can begin the second phase of group process, the conflict phase. During this phase, group members discuss the nature and background of the problem, propose solutions, debate the relative merits of the solutions, and select the best solution or solutions. During the conflict phase, group members begin to clarify their opinions and feelings about the issues. More energy is devoted to sharing differences of opinion, arguing positions, and debating the issues. It is also during this phase that members critically evaluate evidence presented and the reasoning for the solutions proposed. Uneasiness experienced here is called *secondary tension*—the tension caused by disagreement or criticism over one's ideas, evidence, or proposed solutions.

Groups that develop a safe, supportive social dimension during the orientation phase are more likely to successfully weather the secondary tension experienced during the conflict phase. Groups that have not devoted sufficient time to the orientation phase can buckle under the pressures of conflict. Also, groups that have developed an overly cohesive social dimension might see conflict as a threat to their tight-knit, happy family and will avoid the conflict that is necessary to be effective in the task dimension.

3. Emergence.   During the third phase, group members move from debate and conflict to a possible solution that is acceptable to all members. It's a time when the group negotiates, compromises, and begins to discover common ground. Whereas the conflict phase emphasizes differences of opinion, the emergence phase focuses on similarities. During this phase, decisions emerge. Members increasingly make statements of agreement, acceptance, and approval and then decide on or adopt a solution.

4. Reinforcement.   The final phase occurs when group members congratulate themselves on a job well done. During this time, the group also constructs an implementation plan and timetable for the agreed-upon solution. The social dimension is reinforced in this phase with the expression of positive feelings about the group and its accomplishments. Members often feel a strong sense of group identity and belonging. Disagreement, conflicts, and arguments were successfully negotiated and the group is stronger, more effective because of it.

If you've ever worked in small groups, however, you know that they rarely follow the steps Aubrey Fisher identified. A group may go through these phases for each issue it addresses. One group might devote the majority of its time to orientation and socializing, whereas another group will bypass orientation altogether and focus solely on the task at hand. Groups can get sidetracked, abandon their discussion, or disband as a group altogether. In real life, the journey a problem-solving group takes is much more complex and the stages it experiences are not as clearcut as one might hope.

Multiple Sequence Model of Group Development: Perspective 2

To take this complexity into account more accurately, Marshall Poole in 1981 described group development differently. Rather than a linear model, he proposed a multiple sequence model of decision emergence. This model of group process envisions a group moving along three activity tracks—task, relational, and topic. The task track is the task dimension with its procedures and activities. The relational track is the social dimension of the group. And the topic track is the content discussion of group members.

In this model, groups do not necessarily move along these three tracks at the same rate or in the same way. Some groups invest a great amount of time on the relational track before moving to the task track, while other groups may focus primarily on the task track and devote minimal time to the relational track. Breakpoints are the transitions when groups switch activity tracks. In contrast to the linear, step-by-step model proposed by Fisher, the multiple sequence model is much more circular and flexible—more accurately describing the process of group decision-making.

REDISCOVERING YOUR ORIGINAL
GROUP—THE FAMILY

This chapter examined the elements of a small group, the group as a system, and some fundamental characteristics of groups. As we end this chapter, you'll find it beneficial to revisit your family of origin.

Yes, Mom, Dad, and brothers and sisters, if you have them.

Having coached work groups in industry, participated in countless committees at the college and in the community, and guided numerous families in counseling, I am convinced that we, as grown adults, often resort to childhood patterns of communication learned early on in our family of origin. Although we can be surprisingly sophisticated and well mannered when things are going well, we often resort to old patterns of dysfunctional communication when experiencing substantial conflict or pressure within a group setting.

A brief inquiry into your family of origin—feelings you had about your family, the rules of your family, and the expectations your family held about you—will help you understand your current communication behavior with others in small groups. For some, this look back to the family will be nostalgic, amusing, and even enjoyable. For others, recalling those earlier times will be difficult, disturbing, and even painful. Take a few minutes to complete and consider your responses to the following exercises.

INDIVIDUAL AND GROUP EXERCISES

Exercise 1.1   Old Family Photos

Get the old photo album from the shelf and thumb through it. Look at pictures of you and your family when you were 10 years old and younger. Take a closer look at those early family photos. What activities were photographed? What people? What does your face express? Are you happy, sad, lost, confident, etc.? After considering these questions, list five thoughts or feelings you have about your family.

1. _____

2. _____

3. _____

4. _____

5. _____

What feelings or thoughts came to you as you looked at those old photos? Feelings and thoughts about our family of origin often influence and color our expectations, experiences, and even behavior in small group interactions. So it's important to consider them.

Exercise 1.2   Family of Origin Rules

Consider what your life was like growing up in your family of origin. Did your parents plaster rules to the refrigerator and the bathroom mirrors? Did you receive long lectures about what to do and what not to do? Or did your parents even talk to you? Make a list of five spoken (explicit) or unspoken (implicit) rules or norms of behavior you remember from your family of origin. Be as specific as possible.

1. _____

2. _____

3. _____

4. _____

5. _____

Could you list five rules from your family of origin? What did you think of them? What did you think of them when you were a kid? Do you still operate under these communication rules as an adult? As you examine the rules you listed, do you see any that might interfere with how you communicate today?

Exercise 1.3   Group Problem-Solving Permission List

Read each of the following statements pertaining to some aspect of communication or interaction in small group problem-solving. Then indicate whether you agree or disagree with the statement using the ratings below. Respond to each statement based on what you think about your communication behavior, not on what others have said.

(1=strongly disagree, 2=disagree, 3=unsure, 4=agree, 5=strongly agree)

I give myself permission to…

1. participate in a small problem-solving group.	1 2 3 4 5
2. share my thoughts and ideas with the group.	1 2 3 4 5
3. share my feelings with the group.	1 2 3 4 5
4. disagree with other group members.	1 2 3 4 5
5. listen to the opposing ideas of other members.	1 2 3 4 5
6. listen to criticism from other members.	1 2 3 4 5
7. respond to criticism from other members.	1 2 3 4 5
8. consider points of view different from my own.	1 2 3 4 5
9. compromise when it will benefit the group.	1 2 3 4 5
10. facilitate negotiation within the group.	1 2 3 4 5

How did you rate yourself on these 10 statements? You need to discover how you feel about each behavior if you work in a problem-solving group for any length of time. And it's necessary for you to think about each item before you enter into any group process.

Exercise 1.4   Sharing in Your Group

In your small group, share your findings to Exercise 1.3. Prepare a one- or two-minute statement summarizing your response to this exercise; highlight three personal strengths and three weaknesses you see in yourself. When others share their responses and lists, refrain from judging or evaluating them. Simply listen and learn.

T W O

DISCOVERING YOURSELF

Knowing the self is enlightenment.
–Lao Tsu

The morning sun feels warm on my face. There is no sound, no movement. Only this gravel road stretching in a straight line for 20 miles in either direction, like a gray ribbon disappearing into the distance. I'm sitting on the tailgate of my pickup, listening to the silence of the desert, somewhere between Tonopah, Nevada, and the Utah border.

This is my second day in the desert. Last night I camped about three miles from here, on a smooth ridge overlooking this valley. Most of the evening I sat in my beach chair and gazed at the stars overhead. I made no fire. Played no music. I simply sat and watched the stars, as the gentle breeze came up from the southwest. And I listened to the silence all around.

I find the desert silence beautiful. Like a celestial choir from a distant galaxy, its anthem speaks to my heart, calms my body, and once again I hear my own breathing deep and true. I soon discover my thinking ceases and my heart expands to greet the silent stars above.

It is the solitude of the desert that puts me in touch with myself. Far from the responsibilities of family and friends, work and community, I can sit and breathe. And do nothing for a period of time.

Once or twice a year I venture into the desert alone for two or three nights. Leaving the comfort of my wife and children, and all that is familiar, I withdraw from my regular life. The experience replenishes my spirit. It makes me feel whole, alive, and connected to those things that give my life meaning upon my return.

The desert experience also enables me to detach a little more from my usual tendency to want to control others—especially the students I teach in group work, the families I work with in counseling, and the trainees at seminars I conduct in industry. I've discovered that I return from the desert with a stronger desire to watch the process of the group unfold, rather than force my own agenda. I am more willing to listen to the opinions and feelings of others, rather than advocate or advance my own position, because I have gotten in touch with a quieter, deeper part of who I am. The part of me that isn't rattled or shaken by debate, disagreement, criticism, or conflict. And this enhances my ability to face the rigors and requirements of small group problem-solving.

In this chapter we will be exploring you! We'll examine being open to self-discovery, spending time by yourself, and accepting yourself and others. Let's begin with why it's important for you to know yourself.

WORKING IN GROUPS ISN'T EASY

One important lesson I've learned from my experience with groups is that working with a small group in a problem-solving setting is one of the most demanding activities we perform. I believe there are three primary reasons for this. First, very few of us receive any training in group problem-solving. Second, most of us enter into a group problem-solving effort with little or no communication skills training. And third, the majority of us possess a minimal awareness of who we are, what's important to us, and where we're going. These factors often make our group interaction volatile and counterproductive when the group encounters stress or conflict.

At one level, this book is about communicating and interacting with other group members in a positive, constructive manner. At a different level, however, this book is designed to give you the opportunity to discover many wonderful and powerful things about yourself. These new skills, knowledge, and ways of seeing yourself will improve your professional as well as personal life. Each chapter will provide you with the opportunity to practice, develop, and implement many new communication skills in a small group setting. Equally important, you may discover that these same skills will enable you to become a more powerful, compassionate, and giving human being. But in order to do so, you must decide to be open to your own self-discovery.

BEING OPEN TO SELF-DISCOVERY

When was the last time you discovered something new about yourself? Maybe you recently broke off a friendship because you realized you didn't want to invest the energy the relationship required. Perhaps you enrolled in an art class and discovered you really enjoy painting with watercolors. Or maybe you watched a documentary on television and found yourself for the first time in your life thoroughly engrossed in the history of the Japanese samurai warriors.

Every day you have countless opportunities to discover fascinating, beautiful, and even surprising things about yourself. Whether it's the gradual unfolding of a new love or a new appreciation for classical music, you are discovering things about yourself from moment to moment—if you are open.

However, many people are closed to new discoveries about themselves and the world around them. There's an old story about a college professor of religion who visited a Zen priest. The old priest invited the young professor to sit down in his simple yet tasteful room. The professor immediately began talking about Zen. He talked and talked. The old priest began to pour tea into the professor's cup as the young man droned on. Even after the cup was full, the old man continued to pour the tea. The cup overflowed and the tea eventually spilled on the young man's lap.

The professor shouted, "Master, why are you still pouring the tea? Can't you see the cup is already full?"

"You are very observant," replied the priest. "The same is true for you. If you are to receive any of my teachings, you must first empty the cup of your mind, for it is already full of your old learnings."

Like the professor, we too are not always open to self-discovery, or any kind of discovery for that matter, because we are full of old learnings. Old learning can be any idea we have about ourselves and who we think we are. The majority of these ideas came from others—parents, teachers, coaches, friends, and acquaintances. They came from movies, television, radio, magazines, and books, telling us who we should be and what we should want.

Very little of our learning comes from deep within ourselves, because we spend very little of our waking moments completely alone with our thoughts and feelings. We are constantly listening to the television or music. We would prefer the company of just about anyone rather than spend an evening by ourselves.

And besides, what would people think if they saw you eating dinner alone in a restaurant, singing by yourself in a tree house, or venturing into the desert for a couple of days with no company other than the evening stars?

I believe our study of group problem-solving should not begin with an examination of how people behave collectively in groups. Rather, our investigation should begin with an examination of you as an individual. Without a fundamental knowledge of who you are, your interactions with others will lack the connection, depth, and intimacy characteristic of more mature interactions. We need to take time to rediscover who we are. Spending time by ourselves is one way to do this.

SPENDING TIME BY YOURSELF

Not everyone has the desire or the time to go off to the desert for a couple of days of solitude. But I believe there are countless other ways we can experience periods of solitude in our daily lives. Spending time by yourself doesn't necessarily require a solo trip to the Himalayas or joining a Benedictine monastery. Solitude can be discovered right where you are, if you are open to it. Here are some suggestions on simple ways you can experience solitude. Don't feel that you have to try them. But if you'd like to get a feel for who you are without the interruption of others, you might want to try one or two of these activities. I think you'll enjoy them.

Waking Up Earlier

No matter how busy or cramped your life is, you can give yourself the gift of 10 minutes of solitude by waking up earlier in the morning. Experiment with your morning ritual by setting the alarm 10 minutes earlier for one week. Instead of waking up at 6:30, try 6:20. That might not sound too appealing, but you'll discover you're much more flexible than you thought. You can use those extra 10 minutes to sit in the kitchen or living room and watch the sunrise, listen to the birds sing, or hum a song of your own, while the rest of the world sleeps.

Going to Bed Later

Try going to bed 10 minutes later in the evening, especially if you're a night owl. So, instead of going to bed at 11:00, you hit the sack at 11:10. During those extra 10 minutes, you are to do nothing. Bundle up in a big coat and sit in the backyard or on the roof of the house and look at the stars overhead. Don't do anything. Just sit. This is your gift to yourself.

Taking Time Out

During the course of your day, give yourself a 10-minute mini-vacation by taking time-out to stroll around outside of the office or on campus, instead of visiting with your colleagues at the water cooler or the snack shop. This ritual can become the most peaceful and restful 10 minutes of your workday.

Turning Off the Radio

Another way you can be alone is to turn off the radio or stereo (and the cellular phone) when driving to and from work. It's amazing how different your driving experience can be without the constant intrusion of other people's voices and music. In the silence you will hear other things. I think you'll be surprised by the experience.

Stopping for Decompression Time

Returning home from a day at work or school also provides an opportunity to give yourself the gift of solitude. I call it decompression time. Usually, we rush out of work or school, fight the traffic for 30 to 60 minutes, skid into our driveway, and rush into the house, only to be met by family or roommates. We do all this without a quiet transition or decompression time.

Try doing it differently for a while. Before pulling up to your driveway after a day at work or school, you can stop at a nearby park, elementary school, or quiet spot in the neighborhood for 10 minutes to catch your breath, collect yourself, and decompress before entering into the next phase of your daily life. This can transform you back into a pleasant, even charming individual whose arrival at the end of the day will be anticipated with joy!

These are just five simple things you can do to give yourself the gift of solitude. You can probably brainstorm a number of other creative ways to get some time alone. Don't forget the traditional ways of experiencing solitude, like a solo afternoon trip to the lake, an over-night safari, meditation, prayer, or a stroll through the neighborhood after dinner. There are many ways to incorporate a little alone time, and no matter what form of solitude you select, the important point is to get away from the hustle and bustle of life and open yourself to your own music.

I've discovered in my work with problem-solving groups that in-dividuals who experience the greatest amount of disagreement, con-flict, and hostility with others are often those people who are in conflict with themselves. Their relationships with others tell me a great deal about their relationship with themselves.

We need to be at peace with ourselves before we can be at peace with others. One of the best ways to begin this journey is to spend time alone, before entering any group process. Once you've experi-enced solitude, you can begin to discover some things about yourself.

SELF-DISCOVERY INVENTORIES

There are countless ways to discover things about yourself. Personal-ity tests, I.Q. scores, feedback from family and friends, report cards, job reviews, daily horoscope predictions, handwriting analysis, and career placement tests are but a few of the hundreds of methods people use to provide you with information about who they think you are. Advertisements in magazines, billboards, television, and ra-dio, as well as the heroes and heroines in the evening news, movies, and paperbacks, also provide a steady diet of images of who we should strive to emulate if we are to be worthwhile, desirable, and loved. The information from "out there" telling us who we are and who we should be is never-ending.

I want to leave these sources of information that claim to know who you are and who you should be for a moment and have you look to yourself for the same information. Now, I'm not asserting you will know all there is to know about yourself after completing these exercises. But you will become more familiar with yourself by taking a few minutes to answer the questions.

Inventory I: Who Are You?

Complete the following statements with the first idea, noun, adjec-tive, verb, and so on that comes to mind. Don't think about your response, just jot it down. Give yourself only 60 seconds.

1. I am _____.

2. I am _____.

3. I am _____.

4. I am _____.

5. I am _____.

Were you able to write down five responses about who you are? Do you notice any patterns in your responses? For instance, are most of your responses nouns (roles) such as student, wife, Buddhist, engineer, secretary, cowboy, or brain surgeon? Or are most of your responses adjectives such as caring, loving, resentful, lonely, 27 years old, redheaded, or inquisitive? Are there any characteristics or roles you listed that are essential to who you are? Are there any you would like to change or modify? How do you see your responses affecting your interaction with other individuals and groups?

Inventory 2:   What Do You Believe?

Complete the following statements with a belief you hold. Take a bit more time to consider each response than you did in Inventory 1. Give yourself five minutes.

1. I believe _____.

2. I believe _____.

3. I believe _____.

4. I believe _____.

5. I believe _____.

Were you able to write down five beliefs? If not, what does this mean to you? Do you notice any patterns in your responses? Do your beliefs concern yourself, other people, ideas, or things? Are your beliefs stated positively or negatively? If someone held the opposite opinion or belief, how would you feel about the person? If someone held the same opinion or belief, how would you feel about the person? How do you see your beliefs affecting your interaction with other individuals and groups?

Inventory 3: Six Months to Live

Write down five things you would like to do if you discovered you had only six months to live. Assume you will experience no physical pain until the final week of life.

1. _____

2. _____

3. _____

4. _____

5. _____

Do any of your responses surprise you? How do you feel about your responses? Do your responses involve people, places, or things? Which item would you most want to accomplish before dying? If you were going to die in six months, how would that affect your communication with others? How would it affect your attitude toward working with a problem-solving group?

Inventory 4: Your Communication Behaviors

Read the following statements carefully, then circle the number that most accurately describes your response to the statement. Base your response on what you think, not on what others have said about your communication behavior.

(1=strongly disagree, 2=disagree, 3=unsure, 4=agree, 5=strongly agree)

1. I speak in a pleasant tone of voice.	1	2	3	4	5
2. I speak at an adequate rate (speed) of speech.	1	2	3	4	5
3. I speak without verbal fillers ("um," "like," etc.).	1	2	3	4	5
4. I have a relaxed posture when speaking.	1	2	3	4	5
5. I use expressive gestures when speaking.	1	2	3	4	5
6. I smile when I speak with others.	1	2	3	4	5
7. I make eye contact when speaking with others.	1	2	3	4	5
8. I often nod my head in agreement when listening.	1	2	3	4	5
9. I share my opinions with close friends.	1	2	3	4	5
10. I share my opinions with acquaintances/associates.	1	2	3	4	5
11. I share my feelings with close friends.	1	2	3	4	5

12. I share my feelings with acquaintances/associates.	1	2	3	4	5
13. I share my needs with close friends.	1	2	3	4	5
14. I share my needs with acquaintances/associates.	1	2	3	4	5
15. I am comfortable when I disagree with others.	1	2	3	4	5
16. I can disagree without disliking others.	1	2	3	4	5
17. I can verbally admit I'm wrong.	1	2	3	4	5
18. I can ask for forgiveness when I have hurt others.	1	2	3	4	5
19. I make others feel good about themselves.	1	2	3	4	5
20. I am optimistic and positive in my interactions.	1	2	3	4	5

Statements 1 through 3 examine your voice. Statements 4 through 8 look at your nonverbal communication when interacting with others. Statements 9 through 14 examine your ability and willingness to disclose your thoughts and feelings to different people. Statements 15 through 18 focus on your behavior and attitudes when you are in disagreement or conflict with others. They also examine your ability to admit mistakes. And finally, Statements 19 and 20 look at your overall attitude and impact on others. Do you see any categories of communication behavior where you are especially strong? Are there any categories where you are weak or could use improvement? How would your weaknesses affect communication with others in group work? How do you feel about your overall communication skill level?

Inventory 5:   You're Not Perfect

List five communication behaviors, personal habits, personality characteristics, relationships, and anything else you can think of that you feel need improvement. Solicit input from family and friends, co-workers and neighbors. Just the mere fact you would ask others for feedback will change your relationship with them.

1. _____

2. _____

3. _____

4. _____

5. _____

Well, how did you do on this exercise? I hope that you were able to identify five specific weaknesses or shortcomings. Once you can admit you're not perfect and there are things you need to improve, the criticism or threat of criticism from others will have less impact on you. Once you can freely admit to one weakness (or all five!), and not invest great amounts of energy and time defending or denying your weakness, you may experience a new freedom that allows you to be more open to the communication of others.

Inventory 6:   Your Thanksgiving List

List two things you are thankful for about your physical self, two things you are thankful for about your psychological self, and two things you are thankful for about your spiritual self. Choose conditions or attributes you already possess, not those you are striving or hoping to achieve.

1. I'm thankful for my (physical) _____.

2. I'm thankful for my (physical) _____.

3. I'm thankful for my (psychological) _____.

4. I'm thankful for my (psychological) _____.

5. I'm thankful for my (spiritual) _____.

6. I'm thankful for my (spiritual) _____.

Was it easy or difficult to think of six things to be thankful for? If you found it difficult, you may not have taken enough time to be aware of and appreciate all the things that are working in your life. There are countless things about our bodies, minds, and hearts worth appreciating and being thankful for, but we are usually too busy to take time out to marvel at all the wonderful gifts we already possess.

ACCEPTING YOURSELF

Of course, you'll never come to a complete understanding of yourself. It's not possible in this lifetime, and I think a little mystery is good. What's important is that you take the time to ask yourself some important questions about your life every once in a while. Who are you? What do you believe? What are your priorities? How do you communicate to others? What do you want to improve? And what are you thankful for? The six inventories you just completed are invitations for self-discovery. Not for you to consider just once, but rather as a way to stay in touch with yourself in the years to come.

And what do you do with this information about yourself once you discover it? You can become more thankful for the life you have right now. You can have a better idea about beliefs that are important to you and that may guide your decision-making in the future. You can have a greater awareness of your communication behavior and the communication behavior of others. You can have a keener sense of your priorities in life. And you might even be encouraged to improve some weaknesses you identify in yourself.

Knowing yourself—having a sense of who and what you are—is important in your interactions with others in your small group problem-solving activities. It is important for you to have a familiarity with yourself before you enter into group work. You are less apt to look to other group members for approval, for you have already taken the time to examine and accept your strengths as well as your weaknesses. You will be more familiar with your skills, behavior, personality, and maybe even your soul. You will have attempted to accept the good with the bad. That's who you are, and no one's perfect.

I'm not suggesting we neglect or turn a blind eye to those areas we can improve or correct. Just the opposite. I'm suggesting we acknowledge and accept those things we can improve rather than deny or defend their existence. The first step in changing something is to accept its existence.

It's okay to have weaknesses—areas we want or need to improve. When we can acknowledge this in ourselves, we are more likely to accept imperfection in others as well. And accepting others is the first step in working with others. Self-acceptance means we don't have to be perfect.

ACCEPTING OTHERS

We need to accept those who manners irritate us, whose ideas annoy us, and whose goals disturb us. Usually we try to distance ourselves from such individuals. We build walls or fences to keep them out, but in the end we cage ourselves in. More and more, we become prisoners of our own limited and ethnocentric view of the world, when in reality there are countless ways of seeing and experiencing life—ours being just one of the multitude.

The acceptance of others requires us to suspend judgment for a while. This doesn't mean we never evaluate, criticize, or blame. It means we silence our judging, condemning mind for a while and listen to others, even if their ideas are diametrically opposed to ours. It means we become more open to others—to broaden our definitions of what is acceptable, eligible, and tolerable. It means we overlook differences and seek similarities. It means we lighten up and open up to others.

Without this acceptance of others, our interactions in groups can be rigid, intolerant, and blaming. Our relationships with others can be marked by detachment, apathy, and even suspicion, except with those individuals who share our beliefs and goals. Without the acceptance of others, our commitment to the group and our participation in negotiation and compromise will be feeble and insecure. The acceptance of others is crucial to successful group work.

In this chapter we examined the notion of your being open to self-discovery. We looked at ways you could spend time by yourself and we discussed the importance of accepting yourself and others in group communication. Now that you've had an opportunity to discover yourself a bit more, we can begin our examination of the fundamental communication skills for small group problem-solving. Chapter 3 focuses on how to speak to others.

INDIVIDUAL AND GROUP EXERCISES

Exercise 2.1   How Others See Your Communication Behavior

Have someone who knows you well, such as a family member, co-worker, or friend, review your responses to Inventory 4 in this chapter. Briefly explain the inventory. Then have this person comment on your responses to each statement. Withhold judgment as you listen. Let the person talk about how he or she sees you and your communication behavior. Ask for suggestions on how to improve communication. And thank the person for sharing.

Exercise 2.2   Communication Behaviors for You to Improve

Based on the responses you received in Exercise 2.1 and your own thoughtful consideration of your responses to Inventory 4, list three specific behaviors you would like to improve in the future.

1. _____

2. _____

3. _____

Before participating in any future group work or interpersonal interactions, remind yourself about these three behaviors. Make a conscious effort to improve them in the future.

Exercise 2.3   Group Sharing of Individual Communication Behaviors

Make copies of Inventory 4 for members of a group you are currently working with. Ask group members to complete the inventory. When they have finished, make copies of each inventory and distribute them to group members. Distribute your inventory as well. One by one, have group members provide feedback to each member's inventory. This activity can prove very insightful in helping the group communicate more effectively.

THREE

SPEAKING CLEARLY

From his mouth you will know his heart.
–Proverbs

Every time she entered the conference room, the rest of us in the group would cringe, for we knew we'd be in for a long evening.

Janet was one of nine members of an advisory board for a new teacher credential program at a local university. I also sat on the board, which met once a month to oversee this new program.

Although the other members and I observed the usual norms of communication, Janet seemed to delight in breaking many of the rules. She would interrupt speakers in mid-sentence, criticize anyone who questioned an idea she had advanced, and scowl when others objected indirectly to her behavior.

What disturbed me most was Janet's controlling behavior. She would attempt to dominate the discussion with monologues supporting her position, misinterpret the remarks of others to fit her design, and challenge the chairperson with regularity. In short, Janet was a problem-solving group's nightmare.

For six months she attended those meetings. During the sixth meeting, she conducted herself in her usual domineering manner and many of us offered subtle, and not so subtle, objections to her behavior. I felt sorry for her. And yet, I realized her conduct was detrimental to both the task and social dimensions of the group.

During our break I took a walk out to the parking lot to stretch my legs, and I saw Janet, in tears, hurrying to her car. I could hear her crying as she unlocked her car, not far from where I stood in the shadows of a building. Within a moment or so, I heard her engine roar as she sped out of the parking lot.

Apparently, during the break she and the chairperson had argued about her behavior, and Janet had resigned from the board right then and there. I was told Janet calmly strolled out of the room, without uttering a word to any of the others in the group. That was the last they saw of her.

But I had seen Janet cry.

In this chapter we will explore ways to speak clearly—to communicate effectively using specific, direct language. We will examine communication as a learned behavior, five dysfunctional ways of speaking, the communication process, I-statements, four levels of communication, and guidelines for speaking clearly.

COMMUNICATION IS A LEARNED BEHAVIOR

I've often thought about Janet's tears in the parking lot that Tuesday night so many years ago. Her confident exterior, I thought, hid a troubled, perhaps lonely interior. Over the years I've been haunted by the image of her crying in her car. Did she treat her loved ones in the same controlling way? Were there any loved ones in her life? Had she always been this way? Where did she learn to be so pushy?

Janet, like you and me, learned most of her communication behavior in her family of origin. By the age of five, the fundamental structure of our personality has been established. Also by the age of five, the majority of our daily adult language has been learned and our basic communication patterns have been firmly established.

Can our communication patterns be changed? Yes, I believe they can, and people can learn new ways of speaking, listening, and interacting with others. I've spent 20 years teaching communication courses and have witnessed thousands of students improve the way they speak and listen. I have also been a marriage and family counselor since 1986 and have seen how individuals and families can correct dysfunctional patterns of interaction and replace them with more effective methods of communication. But change is not easy.

Most students in my communication courses and clients in therapy are unaware of their own communication patterns and behavior. They often assume that communication skills are something they're born with—like breathing and walking. They believe they're talking when their mouths are moving and they're listening when their mouths are shut. What could be simpler than that?

The first requirement for improving communication behavior is to increase awareness of our current speaking and listening behavior. The second requirement is to want to improve our communication patterns. And the third requirement is to learn and practice new ways of speaking and listening. Improving your speaking and listening skills is the goal of this chapter and the next one. You cannot participate effectively in a problem-solving group without a minimal skill level in these two areas.

FIVE WAYS NOT TO SPEAK

This chapter examines and helps you practice skills that will allow you to speak in a clear, effective, and nonthreatening manner. Before we begin, however, it is useful to review five ways of speaking that should be avoided. It's just as beneficial to know what not to do, as what to do.

Family therapist Virginia Satir has suggested four dysfunctional communication roles family members can adopt in their interactions with one another. She refers to these four roles as the computer, blamer, placater, and distractor. The computer is the cool, collected, intellectual family member who uses logic and reasoning as the primary method of communicating. The blamer is the family member who finds fault and casts blame on others. The placater is the peacemaker who tries to avoid or diffuse conflict at all costs by complying with the wishes of others. And the distractor is the one who attempts to get the focus off the conflict issue, using humor or irrelevant communication to accomplish the task. This is a simplified explanation of Satir's communication roles, but it presents a valuable means for examining communication patterns.

I've constructed a modified version of Satir's model. In my work with families in therapy and in my consulting with work groups in high-tech industry, I have noticed five dysfunctional communication roles: controller, blamer, pleaser, distractor, and ghost. Upon examining these five roles and their characteristic patterns of behavior, you might recognize some aspects of yourself.

The Controller

The *controller* tries to dominate, regulate, and manipulate the interaction of the group. The controller's verbal communication patterns are usually issuing orders and directives. She tends to give directions and explain the superiority of her ideas and solutions over all others presented. The controller often uses logical appeals and intricate reasoning to get her way. She can be a master of words and persuasion. No matter what methodology she uses, her ultimate goal is to control the group and achieve her objectives.

The Blamer

The *blamer* usually finds fault with others and their ideas and suggestions, although he tends not to offer suggestions of his own. He generally blames others for the group's shortcomings and failures. The blamer casts a shadow of doubt and gloom on solutions the group proposes and is the first to say "I told you so" when a solution fails.

The Pleaser

In my model, the *pleaser* is similar to Satir's placater. The pleaser attempts to avoid all conflict by giving in to the wishes of the others. The pleaser agrees to just about anything the others ask or require. And when a conflict begins to arise, he does whatever it takes to dissolve or neutralize the disagreement. He is generally uncomfortable asserting opinions, defending positions, and sharing feelings. The pleaser backs down rather than fights.

The Distractor

The *distractor* doesn't give in, blame, or control. The distractor's role is to draw or deflect attention away from the issue at hand. When the group experiences stress or conflict, she usually jokes about the situation or redirects the discussion to an unrelated issue or topic. Oftentimes the distractor is just as uncomfortable with conflict as the pleaser, but her method for handling discomfort is different. Whereas the pleaser placates or gives in, the distractor utilizes some avoidance technique to change the subject.

The Ghost

The final dysfunctional role I've encountered is the *ghost*. Just as the word suggests, this group member's participation is nonexistent. Like a silent face in the crowd, this person sits in the group and says nothing or doesn't even show up. He is often labeled the nonperformer, the low-verbal, and the passive-aggressive personality. I simply refer to this person as the ghost, because he is not really there to contribute to the group's efforts.

Do any of these role descriptions sound or feel familiar to you? Do they remind you of someone from your family of origin? A friend or coworker? More important, do you see yourself described in any of these five dysfunctional communication roles? If so, you may want to explore your reasons for these behaviors and consider modifying or eliminating them if they no longer serve a purpose in your life.

These five basic dysfunctional roles will appear from time to time during your work with others in groups. Your awareness and ability to recognize these roles will greatly enhance your understanding and effectiveness in your small group work.

Before we examine the skills necessary to speak in a clear, simple, and nonthreatening style, let's spend a few moments reviewing the basic concepts and components of communication.

THE COMMUNICATION PROCESS

Very few people would welcome the thought of living the rest of their lives in complete isolation from other human beings. The prospect of spending life alone on a desert island or facing the horrors of solitary confinement would be intolerable for many of us. The purpose of life is found in our relationships with others during this lifetime. And the primary way we initiate, develop, and maintain these relationships is through the communication process. *Communication* is the process of sending and receiving messages. It's the give and take of life itself. This process takes two forms—verbal and nonverbal communication. We will explore both, as well as examine the communication process within which they operate.

Verbal Communication

The first form of communication is verbal communication. Verbal communication is all spoken and written communication. These are the words of communication, whether they are being boisterously delivered in a speech or silently read in a book. From the moment you vocalize your first word as a toddler to the last words you utter on your deathbed, your verbal communication is essential in your efforts to live your life. This chapter specifically focuses on verbal communication behavior within the small group, so you can learn ways to communicate and share thoughts and feelings more directly.

Nonverbal Communication

The second form of communication is nonverbal. Nonverbal communication is all communication that is not spoken or written. Although we spend a great deal of our formal education learning to communicate verbally with others through reading, writing, and sometimes even speaking, we rarely receive any specific coaching or training in nonverbal communication. The entire universe of nonverbal messages above, below, around, and through the verbal messages is usually neglected in our formal education, and yet researchers have been telling us for years that nonverbal communication has more impact on us than verbal messages.

Nonverbal communication comes in a myriad of forms and is delivered in immeasurable ways. It's embedded in the clothes you wear, the way you speak, the posture you present, the gestures you use, the facial expressions you flash, or the car you drive. It's your silence, your gentle touch, your downcast eyes, or your deep, relaxed breathing. It's all these things and a thousand others that constitute nonverbal communication behavior. In the chapters to follow, we will examine specific ways to observe, interpret, and utilize nonverbal communication.

The Communication Model

The communication process has six basic components: the source, message, encoding, channel, receiver, and decoding. Each component plays an integral function in the dance of communication.

Source.   The *source* is the originator of the message. Communication begins with the source wanting to communicate a thought or feeling to the receiver. An individual or a nation of individuals can be the source of a message. I am the source of the message you are now reading on this page. Hi!

Message.   The *message* is the thought or feeling the source wants to communicate. This message can be an idea, thought, feeling, or emotion.

Encoding.   Once the source has decided to communicate and selected a message, she must *encode* or convert that thought or feeling into verbal and nonverbal symbols that the receiver will understand. This encoding process is highly complex. The words selected, rate of speech, tone of voice, facial expressions, and body language are determined by the source's relationship with the receiver, purpose, speaking situation, and countless other variables. Once the source selects the verbal and nonverbal cues to communicate the message, the encoding process is complete.

Channels.   A *channel* is the medium by which the message is communicated. A speaker can utilize the channels of sound, sight, smell, touch, and taste to send a message. For instance, if you want to communicate affection to another person, you can utilize a variety of channels or combinations of channels. You can say, "I like you" (sound). You can wink your eye (sight). You might hug the individual (touch). You could send some cookies (taste) you baked to the person. Or you could send a bottle of perfume (smell). Usually, the more channels you utilize, the more impact your message will have on the receiver.

Receiver.   The intended destination of the message is called the *receiver*. The receiver can be an individual or a group of people. Once the receiver hears the words or receives the nonverbal cues from the sender, she must interpret or decode them.

Decoding.   The *decoding* process involves making sense out of messages. The receiver must somehow decipher the language and the nonverbal cues sent by the source so they have meaning. After decoding the message, the receiver (now the source) encodes a return message and sends it on its way.

I-STATEMENTS

Now that we've reviewed the communication model, we can begin exploring the requirements of an effective speaker. The first step in speaking clearly is to learn to use I-statement language. With I-statement language you personally take ownership of your thoughts and feelings. Here are some examples of simple I-statements:

> *I* believe trucks are the most useful vehicles.
> *I* think the 49ers are the best team.
> *I* feel upset by what I heard at this morning's meeting.
> It's *my* opinion that you're correct.

Do you notice how the speaker takes ownership of the opinion or feeling expressed? Do you also notice an I-statement doesn't necessarily have to contain the word I to qualify as an I-statement. For example, "It's *my* opinion that you're correct" shows ownership ("my") even though it doesn't contain the word I.

I-statements provide several advantages. First, when a speaker uses I-statements, the receiver of the message knows who the originator or owner of the statement is. If I-statements are not used, the ownership of the message is often uncertain or overstated.

A second advantage to I-statements is they provide a target for the receiver of the message to respond. If a speaker says, "*Everyone* thinks the 49ers are the best team," the receiver might be less likely to disagree, because the speaker uses the word *everyone* as the source of the message. At a subconscious level, it might be difficult to confront or argue with "everyone" rather than with an individual.

A third advantage to I-statements is that they let you know when people are speaking for others. For instance, the statement "My wife likes to go camping" shows the husband is speaking for the wife.

A fourth advantage to I-statements is that they are more thoughtful statements. Because they show ownership, I-statements force the speaker to weigh his remarks more cautiously. I think (I-statement) it's easier to flippantly say, "*Everyone* really likes you," rather than owning the statement and saying, "*I* like you."

A final advantage to I-statements is that they help prevent blaming others. Many times a speaker uses what is called "you-language" instead of I-statements. The speaker sends "you" messages such as "*You* make me mad" and "*You're* a grouch," directing blame to the receiver of the message. If the speaker were to use I-statements such as "*I* get mad when you call me chubby" or "*I* notice you're not smiling," the tone of the statement is much different. There is less of a blaming and faultfinding tone to these statements. Ownership of thoughts and feelings is the purpose of I-statements.

FOUR LEVELS OF COMMUNICATION

Now that we know how to construct an I-statement, the next step in learning how to speak clearly is to examine the four levels of communication, which are surface talk, reporting facts, giving opinions, and sharing feelings.

Each level of communication contains different levels of information. The surface-talk level merely acknowledges others without really sharing. The reporting-fact level shares information we know can be verified or proven. The giving-opinion level deals with our opinions and beliefs. The sharing feelings level involves our most intimate information—our feelings and emotions.

We are not restricted to communicating at just one level. We can communicate from all four levels of disclosure during the course of one conversation. Let's examine the four levels of communication.

Level 1:   Surface Talk

In this first level of sharing, we keep our conversations to a minimal level of disclosure. The surface-talk level of sharing includes greetings, casual acknowledgment of strangers and acquaintances, chit-chat with a coworker, and so on. The primary goal is to acknowledge another human being without having to provide any personal information about ourselves. Listen to the following surface-level remarks:

> How's it going? / Fine. / How about you? / Fine. /
> Looks like rain, huh. / Maybe. /
> Have a good day. / You too. / Thanks. /

As you can see, there isn't any real disclosure going on in these statements. And that's not bad. Their purpose wasn't to conduct some deep, involved conversation. Both parties were merely acknowledging one another in a socially acceptable fashion.

Surface talk is just another way of saying, "I see you and I want to acknowledge you," and usually nothing more. It's a way of being polite to people we come in contact with. It would be humanly impossible to conduct in-depth discussions with everyone we saw in a given day. And we probably wouldn't want to anyway.

Level 2:   Reporting Facts

The second level of communicating involves the reporting of facts. Reporting the outside temperature, giving directions to a stranger, demonstrating how to tune a carburetor, giving a lecture on the mating habits of moths, providing information about a car you're selling through the papers, and answering questions during an interview are examples of reporting factual information.

Facts are different from opinions in that they can be verified. A thermometer can verify the temperature. A map can verify the directions you're giving. A car manual can verify your directions on tuning a carburetor. Scientific research can verify the information in your lecture. Your tune-up receipts can verify your statements about the car's maintenance history. Your previous employers can verify your information regarding past employment performance. The key to identifying communication at this level is that the content of the messages can be verified or proven. The following statements are reporting facts:

> I weigh 162 pounds.
> I was employed by Apple Computer from 1991 to 1994.
> It rained two inches in San Francisco during December.

At the reporting-fact level, there isn't usually a great deal of personal information being shared. Sure, there could be exceptions, such as "I've been in a mental hospital for 20 years," but the majority of factual information reveals little concerning your personal opinions or feelings.

Level 3:   Giving Opinions

Giving opinions is a little more risky than surface talk or reporting facts. By giving your opinions about topics, people, or events, you are exposing more of who you are. You are allowing others to see more of you by sharing your opinions, attitudes, and beliefs with them. This level is much more threatening to you, because there is a greater chance of disagreement, disapproval, and conflict brought about by opinion differences with others.

But disagreement is natural. We couldn't possibly agree on every topic we discuss with others. And once again, we wouldn't want to. That's the beauty of life. It's often our differences that make people interesting to us. They complement our weaknesses and show us new ways of seeing, thinking, and feeling. The following statements are giving opinions:

> It's my *opinion* gun control would not lower violent crime.
> I *know* this plan will work.
> I *believe* if we go to counseling, we'll continue our relationship.

Level 4:   Sharing Feelings

The deepest level of communication is the sharing of feelings. It's at this level two people really communicate for connection—the feeling level. Sharing feelings can be extremely beneficial in your communication with a problem-solving group, because it directly invites discussion about the social dimension of the group.

Many difficulties experienced in the social dimension of the group could be avoided if individuals would be more willing to share their feelings before anger, resentment, or hurt got in the way of effective communication.

Here's a list of feeling words to get you in the mood. This feeling list can provide you with a richer look at the emotional world in which you live. Have fun!

accepted	edgy	intense	restless
afraid	elated	intimidated	sad
annoyed	embarrassed	irritable	sensual
anxious	enthusiastic	jazzed	sentimental
ashamed	ecstatic	joyful	shaky
bashful	excited	lonely	shy
bewildered	fearful	moving	silly
bitter	foolish	mean	strong
bored	free	miserable	subdued
brave	frustrated	needed	tender
calm	furious	neglected	tense
confident	glum	nervous	terrified

Sharing feelings is the most intimate way we can verbally connect with others. It provides others with information about our hearts— our joy, our fear, our anger, and our love. Without this information, we are merely two-dimensional stick figures who never reveal the deeper dimensions of who we are.

GUIDELINES FOR SPEAKING CLEARLY

Now that you know how to make I-statements and communicate at four levels of disclosure, consider these guidelines for speaking clearly:

Be Specific, Not Vague

When speaking, try to use specific language. A common mistake is to assume the listener will receive the same picture in her head that you have in yours when you communicate a word.

When I say, "I see a dog," you hear my sentence and decode the meaning of my words. The word *dog* is a relatively abstract, vague term. The dog you "see" in your head could be big, small, shaggy, or short-haired. You could "see" a bulldog, a collie, or a mutt. What I saw in my mind, and intended to communicate, was a German shepherd. Notice the difference between your picture and mine?

Use specific language to communicate what you think and feel to others. It will prevent a great deal of misunderstanding in your interactions with others.

Communicate Observations, Not Inferences

Observations refer to what your five senses have gathered: what you have seen with your eyes, heard with your ears, smelled with your nose, felt with your fingers, and tasted with your tongue. Inferences, on the other hand, go beyond what you have observed and make assumptions about what you think and feel. Notice the difference between the following observation and inference statements:

> That couple is in love. (inference)
> The two people are walking arm in arm. (observation)

Communicate about a Behavior, Not the Person

It's important to communicate about a person's behavior, rather than comment on what you imagine he is or what he is like. Use adverbs (relating to actions) to describe people rather than adjectives (relating to qualities). Communicating in this way is more specific by reporting behaviors rather than attempting to label the person. Notice the difference in the following statements:

> Harvey is a loudmouth. (describes person)
> Harvey has been talking for 10 minutes. (describes behavior)

Communicate in Terms of "More or Less," Not "Either–Or"

We tend to use polar terms when communicating with others. It was either the most wonderful event or the worst event. Either she was smart or she was stupid. Our laziness often displays itself in our communication. Rather than force descriptions of people, places, and things into extreme terminology with "either-or" language, try to communicate in terms of degree ("more or less" language). For example, rather than saying, "Terry is the loudest person on earth" (either loudest or softest), you could restate your opinion: "Terry speaks louder than Kevin" (matter of degree).

Share Ideas, Don't Give Advice

Avoid the tendency to evaluate and give advice to others. Rather, communicate the sharing of ideas and alternatives instead of giving advice and solutions. For example, instead of saying, "You should get a divorce" (advice), you could suggest, "There are a number of things you can do to improve your marriage, such as take a vacation, enroll in a communication class, or enter into therapy" (suggesting options). This approach lets the other person consider and decide for himself. It also allows the person to save face rather than be proven wrong and be instructed by you.

Communicate What Was Said, Not Why It Was Said

Try not to assess motive or reasoning behind what another person says. Once again, this gets us into the area of inference and assumption. Instead, focus your communication on observable information introduced by such language as "what, how, when, and where." This will keep the discussion on a level that is more effectively communicated and debated, rather than entering into the domain of motive and assumptions.

Match Nonverbal and Verbal Communication

When speaking, try to match your voice, body, and gestures with the content of your verbal message. Mixed messages—inconsistent nonverbal and verbal messages—confuse the listener and threaten clear communication. When you say, "I enjoy spending time with you," your face, voice, and body should also communicate the same message with a smile, cheerful voice, and a relaxed and open body posture.

Keep these seven suggestions for clear communication in mind when you work in your problem-solving groups. You will discover that your communication, as well as your thinking, will be more specific, congruent, and nonthreatening.

This chapter examined five dysfunctional ways of communicating, the communication process, I-statements, four levels of communication, and guidelines for speaking clearly. You will benefit by using specific, direct, and nonthreatening language in your interactions with others.

INDIVIDUAL AND GROUP EXERCISES

Exercise 3.1   Family of Origin Communication Roles

Think back to your family of origin and see if you can identify who played the roles of controller, blamer, pleaser, distractor, or ghost during times of stress or crisis. Identifying family members and their roles is not meant to blame them, but to discover patterns of behavior—theirs and yours. Write their name(s) beside the dysfunctional communication role.

1. Controller: _____   _____

2. Blamer: _____   _____

3. Pleaser: _____   _____

4. Distractor: _____   _____

5. Ghost: _____   _____

Did your family members fit any of the dysfunctional communication roles? Did some play more than one role? What, if any, role(s) did you play within the family? Do family members still play these roles?

One important discovery you can make is the role you played (or still play) in your family of origin. Because if you did, there's a good chance you play a similar role when working in groups. A controller in the family will often try to control others in groups. Likewise, a pleaser in the family will often try to please others outside the family. Be aware of the roles you play when you communicate with others.

Exercise 3.2   Making an I-Statement to Two People

This chapter discussed I-statements and levels of communication. The assumption is that disclosure of your thoughts and feelings is important for others in their attempts to work with and understand you. It's even more important for you to get a sense of who you are. You achieve this sense of self-intimacy, paradoxically, by sharing your thoughts and feelings with others, not by holding them in or hiding them from the listening ear of others.

List two individuals from your personal or professional life you'd like to communicate a thought or feeling to, but haven't had the courage or the opportunity to do so yet. These can be positive or negative thoughts or feelings. Write the name of the person and then briefly note what you would share with them (one sentence only).

Name: _____

Message: _____

Name: _____

Message: _____

How did you feel writing these thoughts or feelings down? What do you think or feel as you see these messages on the page before you? Would you ever consider sharing these messages with the people you listed? If yes, when will you share with them?

Exercise 3.3   Group Role-Play

Have your group make plans for a hypothetical group vacation. Determine where the group will go, how long you will stay, and how much money you will need. What rules will be observed for fun and safety? Finally, decide on a vacation theme.

As the group discusses this topic, have each member role-play one of the five dysfunctional roles: controller, blamer, pleaser, distractor, and ghost. As you talk, stay in your role. If you have more than five group members, have the remaining people role-play themselves. After three minutes of discussion, switch roles and resume talking. Continue to switch dysfunctional roles every three minutes, until the discussion questions are answered.

Discuss what it felt like to play these different roles. Was there a role you felt uncomfortable playing? Was there a role you felt comfortable playing? How did it feel to interact with others when they were playing their roles? How did the role-playing affect the discussion? What did you learn from this experience?

F O U R
LISTENING FOR UNDERSTANDING

**No one can develop fully without feeling
understand by at least one person.**
–Paul Tournier

The oak log crackles and snaps in the fireplace as the orange
flames dance softly above the wood. I stare into the fire, feeling
its heat on my face and hands. We both sit silently in overstuffed
chairs, while an occasional red ember shoots out from the fire and
bounces onto the stone floor in front of us.

Being here in this small, rustic cottage feels good to me. The warm,
golden glow from two kerosene lanterns, and the sound of the crack-
ling fire soothe me, as a light winter rain falls outside. But what feels
best is the way Winston listens to me.

Winston has been my friend and mentor now for 20 years. I trust
his counsel. I appreciate his friendship. But most of all, I like being
heard by him—to be understood at the deepest level.

I've come to this cottage to talk to Winston. Or rather, to be heard
by him. You see, Winston has that rare ability to listen for understanding—to listen without interruption, evaluation, or advice.

When Winston senses I need to be heard, he listens with an acceptance of who I am—not what he wants me to be.

When he listens to understand, I can hear myself think. He doesn't
interrupt my story with his story. He doesn't pass judgment, offer
criticism, or give advice. He won't even try to rescue, teach, or assist.
Winston simply sits and listens in silence. And when he does speak,
he'll ask a question. His questions invite me to explore and discover;
not defend, justify, or even explain. Like a mirror, he lets me see
myself. And I am better because of it. I'm a better husband, father,
teacher, and therapist because he has listened for understanding.

In this chapter we'll examine the skill of active listening—a method of listening for understanding—so you can make others feel understood when they speak to you. We'll also look at ineffective ways to listen, ways to listen for understanding, and guidelines for active listening.

THE IMPORTANCE OF LISTENING

To develop fully as a human being, you need to be heard and understood by at least one person. You need to be in the presence of someone who accepts you for who you are, not for who you may become. You need to be able to share your soul in his or her presence, without fear of rejection, humiliation, or criticism. You must be able to disclose your highest dreams as well as your deepest fears. Without this experience of being heard and understood at the deepest level, you will never fully discover who you are.

Who listens to you when you need to bare your soul? Who listens to you when you need to survey the interior landscapes of your mind and spirit without the imposition of their beliefs, values, or frame of reference? Who listens to you?

I hope you have a special person or two in your life who provides this gift of listening for understanding. So much of what passes for listening these days is actually judging the correctness of your statements, matching the content of your story with a better story, or bestowing upon you advice and counsel. Worse yet, many people don't even attempt to listen to what you say or selectively listen to only those topics that interest them. Some will even pretend to listen while they're busy formulating their response to what you're saying.

FOUR WAYS NOT TO LISTEN

Before we examine the skill of listening for understanding, let's take a moment to review four ways not to listen. They are nonlistening, listening to ignore, listening selectively, and listening for the ego.

Nonlistening

At the lowest level of listening, you don't listen at all. In fact, you forbid any kind of talking or sharing. The common command is simply "Shut up." Variations of this are: "I don't want to listen to you," "Don't tell me your problems," and "Tell someone else."

If this style of listening (really nonlistening) is chronic, very little communication or connection can occur. There are rare occasions when it might be necessary to forbid talking. But as a rule, this is not a healthy way to communicate with others, especially in problem-solving groups when the input of all members is valued.

Listening to Ignore

With this style of listening, the listener pretends to be listening, but is not really receiving the messages from the speaker. The common response with this level of listening is "That's nice dear." Variations of this are "Yeah, I hear you," "Whatever you say," and "Okay, okay! I heard you." The result of this listening style is that no real listening is taking place, although the listener verbally acknowledges the speaker. Being heard at this level can be even more frustrating for the speaker than the nonlistening style because although the listener offers some verbal agreement, both parties understand that little or no listening is occurring. At least at the nonlistening level, the "shut up" level, no attempt at deception is being made. And the conflict is out in the open.

Listening Selectively

At this level, the listener hears only what he wants to hear. He selectively sifts through the many words of the message and hears only those things he wants to hear or is comfortable hearing. The rest of the message goes out the other ear. Although this level of listening is normal to some degree, we must beware of it when we are discussing vitally important issues or are in a conflict. When clear communication is essential, selective listening interferes with sending and receiving messages.

Listening for the Ego

In the fourth, most common style of listening, the listener imposes her ego on the speaker. After the speaker has made a statement, the listener evaluates the rightness or the wrongness of the statement according to what she thinks and believes. The listener judges the statement as good or bad using her criteria and gives advice she feels is helpful. The listener does a million and one things with the speaker's statement, but always from her point of view. Everything that occurs in this style of listening finds its origins in the listener—her values, her beliefs, and her life.

In this style, all listening is filtered through the lens of "Does it confirm or disconfirm the listener's point of view?" The listener takes everything that is communicated very personally. All messages communicated to him either agree with what he thinks and feels, or they do not. If they do, great! All is well in the universe. If they don't, there's trouble! He needs to go to war immediately in his next sentence—he needs to disagree, punish, debate, humiliate, persecute, reeducate, or advise in order to impose his ego on others. And this is exactly how most of us listen the majority of our waking hours.

This fourth style makes true listening—listening for understanding—impossible. At this level, we conduct our listening with our judge's robe on and gavel in hand. We listen to confirm ourselves, not to understand others. Understanding isn't the goal of this style of listening. Winning is.

LISTENING FOR UNDERSTANDING

In the four ways not to listen, the focus was on the listener. First, he didn't want to listen, so he simply forbade the speaker from talking. Second, he pretended to listen, but he wasn't really paying attention to the speaker. He simply dismissed the speaker with superficial agreement. Third, he heard only what he wanted to hear, and ignored or forgot the rest of the message. And fourth, he listened to impose his ego on the speaker.

Now comes a unique way of listening—a style that is very different from the four styles of nonlistening. When you listen for understanding, the spotlight shifts from the listener to the speaker. The speaker is now the center of the stage, and the listener is now off-stage. No longer is the listener's ego of primary importance. It now becomes secondary to the speaker's ego.

The primary goal of listening for understanding is to discover how the speaker thinks and feels. What does she experience, desire, need, and want? How does the world look from her unique perspective? What does it mean to be her, in her world?

This kind of listening—listening for understanding—is how therapists, psychologists, and psychiatrists are trained to listen to their clients. And that's the way our group members need to be heard by us at times. They need to be listened to for understanding.

The secret to listening for understanding is to test the accuracy of your message reception. The meaning of messages is not in the words of the message, but rather in the person sending the message and in the person receiving the message. In other words, meaning is in people, not in words. For example, the word *ball* can mean a football to me, a fun time to you, and a formal dance to someone else. The symbol or word *ball* was the same for all three of us, but the meaning we individually assigned to that word was very different. Meaning is not in words, but in people.

So, one of the most important goals of effective communication is to make certain that the picture (message/meaning) the source has in his head is the same one you reconstruct in your head. That's the great challenge of communication—the negotiation of meaning.

Active listening is a technique that provides us with a simple way of making sure that the message we receive is the message the source intended. It's the way we listen for understanding. Active listening is telling the speaker what the message means to you. It gives you the opportunity to prove to the source of the message that you understood the ideas and feelings he was attempting to convey. And it also gives the source of the message the opportunity to confirm or clarify your interpretations. In essence, active listening is the process of listening for understanding.

There are four basic steps to the active listening process. If you follow these simple steps, you'll have mastered one of the fundamental skills of effective communication—listening for understanding.

Active Listening: A Four-Step Process

Step 1. Speaker makes statement.

Step 2. Listener paraphrases speaker's statement.

Step 3. Speaker accepts paraphrase ("Yes, that's what I meant.") or rejects paraphrase ("No, that's not what I meant.")

Step 4. If rejected, speaker repeats Step 1.

   If accepted, listener free to express thought/feeling.

Here is an example of active listening—listening for understanding.

Ann: I want to enroll in another class after the semester is over.

Jason: *Are you saying you enjoy going to school?*

Ann: Not really. It's just that I want to quit selling real estate and maybe teach art in a high school.

Jason: *So, you want to get your teaching credential someday?*

Ann: I'd love to. I know teachers don't get paid much, but I wouldn't mind.

Jason: *You're saying you love teaching for the sheer joy of it?*

Ann: Yes, that's exactly how I feel.

Do you notice how the active listener is telling the speaker what the message means to him? Jason does did not try to impose his ego on Ann by evaluating, judging, giving advice, or moralizing. He simply paraphrases or reflects back to Ann what he thinks she meant. An easy way to remember the essence of active listening is to imagine yourself as a mirror reflecting the message back to the speaker. The goal of active listening is to verify understanding.

Active Listening: You Technique

The most basic form of active listening is mirroring back to the speaker the content of the message with a question beginning with the word *you*. Here are some examples of active listening questions that use the You Technique:

Terri: This is the third time I've been turned down for a promotion.
Juan: *You* feel pretty disappointed?
Terri: I sure do.
Zak: I can't believe I'm actually painting pictures that look like real seascapes! And it's only my fifth art class!
Alana: *You're* feeling pretty proud of your rapid progress?
Zak: You bet! I never thought of myself as an artist.

Active Listening Questions

In addition to the simple You Technique of active listening, you can use the following phrases in your attempts to reflect the speaker's statements:

Do you mean...?   Are you saying...?   Do I understand you to say...?
Are you feeling...?

Here is an example of active listening questions:

Sherry: The history exam was more than I expected.
Cora: *Are you saying* the exam was difficult?
Sherry: No, it just covered more material than I thought it would.

Active Listening Statements

You can also use statements that serve the same function as active listening questions. Note the following opening phrases:

I hear you saying...   What you're saying...   What you're feeling is...
I understand you to mean...   It sounds like you...   I'm feeling that you...

Whether you use the You Technique, active listening questions, or active listening statements, the purpose is always the same—to verify understanding of the speaker's statements. This is the initial step in all communication: to make certain the picture (message) you decode is the picture (message) the speaker encoded or intended. When you listen for understanding, your sole purpose is to ensure the pictures match. Sounds simple, but we rarely listen with this in mind.

Advantages of Active Listening

Active listening has a number of advantages. First, and most obvious, it proves understanding. It assures both speaker and listener the message sent was indeed the message received. That is what is meant by listening for understanding.

Second, active listening involves the listener. No longer does the listener passively sit and assume he has received the message accurately. He must participate in the process of communication and become involved in the message negotiation.

Third, active listening relieves the listener from having to act as judge, teacher, or rescuer. The listener simply reflects the message back to the speaker, but doesn't problem-solve, judge, give advice, or perform a hundred other activities listeners are often inclined to do.

Fourth, the speaker has a safe place to disclose thoughts and feelings without being threatened, criticized, or punished. The speaker can share, explore, and consider her thoughts and feelings without fear of evaluation.

Fifth, active listening develops trust between the speaker and the listener. It isn't very often an individual is given the opportunity to share what's really on his mind or deep in his heart without being attacked, rejected, or rescued. This is the most important reward of listening for understanding. The speaker trusts you.

GUIDELINES FOR ACTIVE LISTENING

Now that you have a basic understanding of how to use these simple techniques of active listening, I would like to suggest some guidelines that will help you listen for understanding.

Avoid Parroting

A common problem the beginning active listener makes is to paraphrase, word for word, the speaker's statement. Just like a parrot, the listener will reflect verbatim the words of the speaker. Here are a couple of examples of parroting:

Hector: I feel happy.

Sam: *You feel happy?*

Sally: I'm have second thoughts about leaving.

Tim: *You're having second thoughts about leaving?*

The main disadvantage to parroting is that the listener doesn't prove true understanding of the speaker's statement. He merely repeats the exact wording of the statement and does not process the statement into his own words. A second disadvantage of parroting is the "echo" effect, which quickly becomes tiring to hear. Be creative! Put the speaker's statement into your own words.

Avoid Overuse of Active Listening

Nothing is more irritating than having someone use active listening to mirror every statement you make during a conversation. This can drive people crazy. You should reserve active listening for those occasions when (1) you need to clarify the speaker's message, (2) the speaker needs to feel understood by you, (3) the speaker needs to vent or process feelings, or (4) you and the speaker are in conflict.

If you use active listening about once every five statements you make during a conversation, you will not only improve the quality of the communication, you will also dramatically improve the quality of your relationships.

Avoid Inappropriate Active Listening

Sometimes active listening is inappropriate. Although there are no fast and easy rules on when it is inappropriate to use active listening, you'll soon get a gut feeling after you've practiced it awhile. Here are some obvious examples of when it would be inappropriate to use the understanding response:

Ann: What time is it, Omar?

Omar: *Are you asking what time is it?*

Nancy: The house is burning!

Ted: *You're saying the house is burning?*

In each example, the listener inappropriately used active listening. The speaker was making a request or statement that did not require clarification from the listener. If these were real conversations, very few people would blame the speaker if she kicked the listener in the shin!

Listen for Feelings

Active listening is an excellent tool for reflecting the feelings of the speaker, whether they were clearly stated or simply implied. For you to reflect the feeling or feelings you thought the speaker was expressing is the most powerful way you can communicate empathy—the ability to experience what the other person feels.

Listen to the Speaker's Body

In addition to listening to the words of the speaker, you need to pay close attention to the speaker's body. The nonverbal behavior of the speaker is equally important in the communication interaction. What kinds of silent messages are being given off by the speaker's posture, gestures, breathing, eye contact, face, tone of voice, rate of speech, and touch? You need to develop your skill at reading the speaker's body in your attempts to understand what she is trying to communicate to you.

This can be extremely tricky; nonverbal behavior is so difficult to decipher and interpret. Social scientists, who devote their entire lives to unlocking the body's silent messages, haven't yet provided us with clear and easy rules for understanding nonverbal communication. The majority of nonverbal communication is culturally determined and complicated by individual quirks and twitches. I say this to remind you it's difficult to accurately read someone else's nonverbal behavior.

But you can do something. You can ask questions! You can use a form of active listening to invite dialogue about the speaker's feelings by describing a nonverbal behavior of theirs, followed by an active listening question. Here are some examples:

> I see that you're smiling again. Are you pleased?
> You're speaking quickly. Are you feeling rushed?
> You just threw the television out the window. Are you upset with me?

Many times the speaker is unwilling or unable to verbally share a feeling with you, but her nonverbal behavior is communicating that feeling nonetheless. This technique enables you to comment on the behavior and to open dialogue about feelings. There are times when the speaker isn't consciously aware of a feeling he possesses, but his body is still communicating the feeling to you. In such instances, you can be helpful in getting him in touch with his feelings by using this simple technique.

Don't be concerned about being correct or incorrect regarding your guesses about the speaker's feelings. Your purpose is to reflect her nonverbal behavior and show an interest in her feelings. You're not supposed to be a mind (or heart) reader. You are just someone who is interested in understanding the speaker's feelings.

In this chapter we examined the skill of active listening—a method of listening for understanding—so you can make others feel understood when they speak to you. We also looked at four ineffective ways of listening, three variations of listening for understanding, and guidelines for active listening. Your listening skills are essential to effective communication in groups. A good rule of thumb to keep in mind is to listen with question marks and not exclamation marks.

INDIVIDUAL AND GROUP EXERCISES

Exercise 4.1   Listening the Wrong Way

The next time you're talking with a friend, try listening the wrong way—a nonunderstanding listening style. Don't tell your friend what you are doing. Listen for your ego. Judge everything your friend says in terms of whether you agree with her or not. Try not to be too obvious or obnoxious. But in a gentle way, verbally judge the content of what she says during the conversation. See if you can listen the "wrong way" for a minute or two.

Did your friend notice your listening response style? What did she say or do to indicate she noticed your change in listening (at least I hope this isn't your normal style of listening)? How did listening the wrong way affect or modify the content of the discussion? How did listening the wrong way affect or modify the way your friend communicated? How did it feel to you? Did it feel familiar? Did it feel strange? Who listens to you in this style? How does it feel to you to be judged when you share with another? Did the two of you discuss this little experiment after you shared the intent of this experiment? What did you discover about yourself?

Exercise 4.2   Listening for Understanding

With a different friend, try listening for understanding (active listening) during a conversation for four or five minutes. Don't tell your friend about your little experiment. Simply slip into an active listening style of communicating without verbally noting the change. Carry on your part of the conversation. If he asks you a question, reply. But the primary purpose of the experiment is for you to listen in a way that provides you with a greater understanding of what your friend thinks and feels. Use questions or statements that begin with "You're saying...," "You're feeling...," "What I hear you saying is...," "You feel that...?," "Sounds like you...," and so on. Use some variety in your listening for understanding. And don't reflect every statement your friend makes. Try active listening once or twice every minute— that's enough. The rest of the time carry your end of the conversation. See if you can listen for understanding for four or five minutes without letting on that you're experimenting. After the conversation is over, feel free to share with your friend that you were experimenting with a new way of listening—a method that would improve your understanding.

Did your friend notice your listening response style? What did he say or do that indicated he noticed your change in listening? How did listening for understanding affect or modify the content of the discussion? How did listening for understanding affect or modify the way your friend communicated with you? How did it feel to you? What did you discover about yourself as you attempted to listen for understanding?

Exercise 4.3   Group Paraphrasing

In your group, have each member make a statement about how he or she perceives a specific area of weakness in the group's performance (either task or social dimension). Then have the person immediately to the right of the speaker attempt to paraphrase (listening for understanding) the content of the statement to the speaker's satisfaction. If the paraphrase is correct and the speaker says, "That's exactly what I mean!" then the listener makes his or her own statement about a group weakness. If the paraphrase is incorrect, the listener tries a second time. If the second paraphrase is incorrect, then any group member can offer a paraphrase of the speaker's original statement.

How did the exercise work? What made some group members more successful at paraphrasing than others? How did it feel to paraphrase others? How did it feel to be paraphrased by others? How might you use listening for understanding in your group work or personal life?

FIVE
PROBLEM-SOLVING IN GROUPS

**Every problem provides an opportunity
for you to do your best.
–Duke Ellington**

It was two hours into a meeting that seemed to drag on forever. I sat in one corner of the room observing seven men and women, all assembly-line production team managers at a local computer company, discussing the problem of employee language barriers. Some managers had to cope with six different languages in their production crews of 30 individuals.

I was one of a three-member communication consulting team hired to observe three two-hour meetings and then suggest specific ways this group could improve its communication behavior.

After three meetings, the managers had yet to agree on a solution to the problem. Our observation team met later to compare notes and view segments of the videotaped discussions. We made five interesting observations about the group's problem-solving behavior.

First, the group spent a total of only 20 minutes, or 6 percent of the discussion time, analyzing the scope and nature of the problem during the six hours. Second, they used up approximately 2.5 hours, or 42 percent of the time, explaining, clarifying, and defending their own individual proposals. Third, they generated only five identifiable solutions during the three meetings. Fourth, for approximately 80 minutes, or 22 percent of the discussion time, they shared unrelated historical information about the corporation, company gossip, and other topics not directly related to the subject of language barriers. And finally, the group made only six attempts to provide any structure to the discussion in the form of summaries or reviews.

The production managers were surprised by our observations and most astonished by the self-centered nature of each individual's behavior and the group's inability to keep the discussion focused.

In the training that followed, our team (1) showed the managers how to spend considerably more time examining and discussing the problem; (2) coached them to use active listening to clarify the positions of those who criticized their proposed solutions; (3) instructed them on the use of the brainstorming technique to generate many more possible solutions; (4) trained them to identify and limit tangential and irrelevant discussion during the problem-solving process; and (5) taught them verbal tools and strategies they could use to guide, direct, focus, and summarize discussions in a more effective and expedient manner.

Their problem-solving sessions after our training were much more productive, creative, and focused. The eventual solutions to the language barrier problems were far different from the ones they originally proposed. And what was most heartening to us were their increased skills and confidence in working with groups.

This chapter discusses the myths of small group problem-solving, decision-making techniques, discussion questions, the standard problem-solving agenda, and the circular nature of problem-solving itself. Let's begin our exploration with a discussion of some false ideas about small group problem-solving.

MYTHS OF SMALL GROUP PROBLEM-SOLVING

The assumptions we bring into the small group problem-solving process directly and powerfully influence the manner in which we participate and feel about working with others in groups. The following are some myths or false assumptions about small group process.

Myth 1: There Is Only One Solution to a Problem

When a group gets together to solve a problem, there is a tendency for the group to think there can only be one "right" answer to the problem. Maybe this is a carryover from our schooldays, when each question on a quiz or examination had only "one correct answer." But in real life there are many ways to skin a cat. When working in a problem-solving group, don't limit yourself by looking for only one solution to a problem—look for as many as you can. Challenge all group members who feel they have discovered the "right" answer. Always work to broaden and increase the possibilities and solutions. Think big! Think of the many!

Myth 2:   Our Solution Is the Best Solution

Once the group has weathered the storms of the problem-solving process, there is often a feeling or attitude of invincibility or infallibility. Taken to an extreme, this phenomenon is known as *groupthink*—the group attitude that it can do no wrong. We"ll examine the concept of groupthink in a later chapter—but for now, we need to remind ourselves that the assumption that the group's decision or solution is the best, simply because the group invested much effort and experienced much discomfort in its creation, can be false.

The group needs to challenge the myth of "our solution is the best." It would be of greater value for group members to adopt a more tentative attitude or approach to their solution by saying, "This is the best solution we can come up with at the moment. But we are staying open to the possibility of discovering other solutions, maybe even better solutions, in the days to come." This attitude of openness and discovery, rather than arrogance and closed-mindedness, will keep the group healthy, wealthy (in the spiritual sense), and wise.

Myth 3:   Two Heads Are better than One

Getting together with other people to solve problems is based on the notion that "two heads are better than one," and that a group of people can provide more information, experience, and creativity than a single person. But for this to occur, the members must possess some level of mutual respect, cooperation, and skill. There must exist a minimal level of willingness to come together and join forces so their pool of information, experiences, and resources can be shared, built upon, and expanded in a spirit of cooperation.

If this minimal level of willingness, mutual respect, cooperation, and goodwill is not achieved, then the consequences can be harmful, counterproductive, and even disastrous. Working in groups is no picnic, as you are well aware. It exacts a price from each of its members in time and effort. But the benefits outweigh the costs.

Myth 4:   No Conflict Will Arise

Another assumption many people bring to group work is that there should be no conflict during the process of problem-solving. Aren't we grown, mature adults? Aren't we rational, logical people?

Well, we are, and we aren't. I am beginning to think I'm not as rational, logical, and mature as I once thought when I was younger. Especially when I'm working under pressure or during times of extreme stress. The more honest I am with myself in matters like this, the more willing I am to admit to my occasional self-centeredness, my unwillingness to listen, and my reluctance to compromise.

Groups can experience greater conflict after members feel a certain level of security and trust within the group. This is natural. Whenever people share ideas, there will be conflict. This isn't bad; it just comes with the territory. Without conflict, group members cannot create the solutions their problems require. Like labor pains during childbirth, there is no creation without some suffering. The group must experience conflict to be successful.

Myth 5:   I Must Like and Be Liked by Everyone

A tremendous amount of emotional energy is spent on the belief that you should like each group member and that each member should like you, as if this were an invitation to a mutual admiration society rather than a problem-solving group.

I find it useful when interpersonal conflict arises within a group to remember the One-Third Rule. My theory is that in any group of people, one-third of them will like you, no matter what you do. One-third of the people will not like you, no matter what you do. And one-third of the people don't care about you either way, no matter what you do. It would be nice if everyone liked everyone else in the group, but unfortunately such a mutual admiration society doesn't happen often. So don't lose sleep over someone's sneer, snide remark, or personal attack. It comes with the territory. Keep in mind the One-Third Rule and you'll be easier on yourself and on others. You don't have to be liked or approved of by everyone.

Myth 6:   Everything Must Go My Way

There is a subtle, almost unconscious assumption that if things don't go the way you want them to go, you should be disappointed, upset, or even angry. One of the important lessons in life is that you don't always get what you want. In fact, you would most likely be in a terrible mess if every one of your wishes, fantasies, and dreams came true. Can you even begin to imagine the hideous life you would have right now if even half of the wishes you dreamed about during your high school years came true?

An important discovery I make about myself each time I work with a problem-solving group is that my ideas aren't always the best, my suggestions aren't always the most insightful, and my intuitions are often proven wrong. What I find refreshing in working with a group is a renewed sense of humility, practice in letting go of what I think is right and good, and a deeper appreciation for the beauty and creativity of others. I discover I am moved by other human beings in ways that are unexpected and sometimes even profound.

Myth 7: Every Problem Has a Solution

Paradoxically, this final myth contradicts to some extent what was suggested in Myth 1. If there is a problem, there has to be a workable, acceptable solution floating around somewhere in the universe. How can there be a problem without a solution? we think to ourselves. But another concept you may want to challenge is the notion that every problem has a solution. That may not always be the case.

Today, some experts have pronounced their somber judgments that there might be no current solutions to such significant problems as the destruction of the ozone layer, the depletion of the rain forests, the continued pollution of our oceans, and the rise in violent crime. I don't know whether this is true or not, but the possibility remains that there may be no solutions to these particular problems based on our current technology and resources.

Psychiatrist Carl Jung had an interesting thought about the nature of problems. He felt that many problems in life may have no solution. "They might never be solved," he cautioned, "but merely outgrown." Maybe some problems cannot be solved. We merely outgrow them, or lose interest in them.

If you keep challenging these myths about small group problem-solving, you will be a wiser, more effective group participant. In the end, however, you want to do your best in working with others in a problem-solving context, but remember that you have a life beyond this group of people and the problem your group is attempting to solve. Keep things in perspective.

DECISION-MAKING TECHNIQUES

Now that you have the right attitude toward working with others in groups, we can introduce some decision-making techniques.

Each of us makes hundreds of decisions every day. Most of these decisions are relatively insignificant—what shoes to wear, where to go to lunch, whom to call, which gas station to turn into, and when to go to sleep. Other decisions are more significant: Should I leave this job? Can I afford this home? Should I end this relationship? Can I change careers at this age?

When it comes to these more significant life questions, how do you make your decisions? Some people consult horoscopes, while others flip a coin. One person will ask the advice of a parent, while another person will pray for a sign. Others go to a mountaintop and meditate until a direction becomes clear. All these methods, and more, are utilized in our personal decision-making process.

But when it comes to small group decision-making, we do not always have the luxury to consult these more intimate, idiosyncratic methods of making decisions. The small group decision-making process is less private, more public.

That's why we need to review some of the more widely used decision-making techniques. Then you can put your tarot cards in mothballs, at least while you're working in a group. The five most common small group decision-making techniques are decision by the leader, majority vote, compromise, arbitration, and consensus.

Decision by the Leader

This method calls for the leader to decide for the group, either after discussion with the group or without the group's contributions. Traditionally, many American business corporations have made their decisions in this fashion. The advantages of this method of decision-making are that it minimizes wasted time, reinforces the traditional hierarchical business structure, and can be efficient in making administrative decisions. The disadvantages can be a lack of commitment to the solution by the group, superficial or minimal group discussion and analysis, and the development of an adversarial relationship between leader and group members.

A variation of this method includes decision by a designated authority or expert to whom the group defers decision-making authority because the authority possesses more expertise and experience than they might have. Another method is decision by an executive committee or subgroup made up of group members. This method works well if the group is overloaded with work and total group participation is not feasible.

Decision by Majority Rule

The most widely used method of group decision-making is majority rule or voting. We've all experienced the final invitation to conflict resolution when someone in the group yells, "Well, let's vote on it! I'm tired of arguing about this topic!" The vote is taken and the matter is settled. Or is it really?

The disadvantages of majority rule are that there are always winners and losers and that majority rule provides no protection for the minority. Additionally, the losers often suffer because they feel their position was discarded by the majority. Many times, the minority will work to sabotage the implementation of the solution or decision.

The advantages are that decisions can be made quickly and time can be saved. Majority rule is effective for procedural matters, such as voting on meeting times, placement of items on the agenda, and other administrative issues. But decision-making that needs commitment from the entire group requires a different way of deciding.

Decision by Compromise

The decision by compromise method of decision-making is a bartering technique: "If you give us this, we'll give you that." Members of one point of view will give up some aspect of their solution in exchange for support from other group members. Compromise combines aspects of the most popular solutions being discussed.

In theory, compromise doesn't sound all that bad. Isn't life compromise? But in reality, compromise often results in low commitment to the solution, because the solution can be so weakened or diluted as to make it ineffective or unacceptable.

Compromise is good when the position of members representing one point of view is incompatible with those representing the other point of view. Compromise will permit the discussion to continue, whereas lack of compromise would have killed discussion long ago.

The disadvantage to compromise is that it is often used too early in discussion and prevents productive exploration of alternatives. It also produces decisions or solutions that are watered down, "averaging out" differences between various points of view.

Decision by Arbitration

Sometimes decision-making needs to come from outside the group or groups in conflict. For instance, a dispute between labor and management often requires decisions to be made by a third party—

an arbitrator. The *arbitrator* is an impartial third party, whose decision both sides have agreed to be binding. In other words, both groups will accept the arbitrator's decision.

The advantage of this method of decision-making is that the arbitrator will break an impasse or stalemate. Arbitration gets the ball rolling again, whereas an impasse between the two sides could polarize them even more, increase tension and hostility, and prevent compromise from ever occurring. The disadvantage is similar to majority rule. The loser in the decision must accept the ruling of the arbitrator and in doing so must also accept the fate of the minority.

Decision by Consensus

A highly effective decision-making method for a small group is consensus. Consensus requires that all group members find the decision acceptable. The decision may *not* be each member's first choice, but each member regards the decision as acceptable and workable.

Consensus is different from decision by compromise in that the final decision is not an "averaged out," hybrid decision between two different points of view. The decision is a new, third point of view that each group member regards as workable and acceptable.

A test for consensus during group discussion is the question "Can you live with it for a period of time?" not "Is this your number-one choice?" The question is neither "Are you happy with this decision?" nor "Is this the perfect solution?" The question is "Can you live with it for a period of time?" In other words, do you feel the decision is (1) workable and (2) acceptable?

An advantage of decision by consensus is that it increases member satisfaction with the decision, because *all* group members must buy into the decision of the group. *Any* member can prevent or block the acceptance of a decision. So the ultimate decision is the product of thorough discussion. Consensus also promotes a stronger social dimension in the group by increasing cohesion and increases the information base, because discussion cannot be terminated by vote or compromise. Finally, it increases the quality of the decisions.

A disadvantage of decision-making by consensus is that it requires a tremendous amount of time. Whereas the other four methods of decision-making—by leader, majority rule, compromise, and arbitration—can terminate discussion with the imposition of the decision, consensus demands the members talk until they discover a decision that is workable and acceptable to all members.

Guidelines for Reaching Consensus

J. Hall and W. Watson in 1970 suggested these five guidelines for reaching consensus within a group:

1. Don't argue for your own position.   Present your views and positions. Then *listen* to the views and positions of the other group members.

2. Don't assume this is a contest.   Try not to view the discussion as an activity that someone has to win and someone has to lose. Look for the next acceptable option for all members.

3. Don't avoid conflict.   Difference of opinion is natural. Critically listen to and evaluate the arguments and evidence of others. Yield only to the views and opinions that make sense to you. Differences of opinion make for higher-quality decisions.

4. Don't use conflict reducing techniques.   Don't vote, flip coins, compromise, or average. These techniques require someone to win and someone to lose.

5. Include the participation of all members.   Make certain all group members are included in the decision-making process. Ask low-verbal members for their opinions, reactions, and feelings.

DISCUSSION QUESTIONS

One of the most important tools in decision-making and problem-solving in small groups is the discussion question. The discussion question helps in problem identification. Problems need to be formulated into a discussion question to help focus the group's thinking, research, and discussion. As you will see, different types of discussion questions reveal and produce entirely different kinds of decisions and solutions to a problem. The three types of discussion questions are questions of fact, value, and policy.

Question of Fact

A question of fact asks if something is true, if something is occurring, or if something has already occurred. Questions of fact involve who, what, when, where, and why questions. Examples of questions of fact are:

> How much money is spent by our competitors on advertising?
> When did production begin to increase by more than 10 percent annually?
> Who served as group leader during our last meeting?

Questions of Value

Questions of value ask for a judgment on whether something is good or bad, right or wrong. Such questions involve an individual's subjective opinion regarding matters of taste. These questions are more difficult for a group to agree upon, because the values, tastes, and beliefs of each member can be so different. Examples of questions of value are:

Is it good public relations to donate our product to charitable causes?
Is our new design pleasing to the eye?
Who was the best group leader during the last quarter?

Questions of Policy

A question of policy invites discussion regarding what course of action should be taken. Questions of policy are generally the result of a problem or situation needing change or improvement. To answer a question of policy, the group must also answer many questions of fact and value in their problem-solving deliberations. Examples of questions of policy:

What should our policy be toward increased competition in advertising?
What should we do if we increase profits by more than 30 percent annually?
What should our policy be if group leaders don't meet minimal standards?

Questions of policy are the beginning focal point of a group's attempts to solve a problem. The question of policy should be as specific as possible. Vague and general terms must be avoided. Limit your question of policy to only one issue at a time. Multiple-issue policy questions tend to scatter your group's research, energy, and focus. "What should be our hospital's policy toward rising surgical costs, malpractice litigation regarding psychiatric care, and custodial demands for pay raises?" is a question of policy that covers too many issues. A more specific question would be "What should our hospital's policy be toward rising surgical costs?"

THE STANDARD PROBLEM-SOLVING AGENDA

Now that we have a feel for the myths of problem-solving, methods for decision-making, and different types of discussion questions, we can examine the standard problem-solving agenda.

Most current problem-solving agendas are based upon John Dewey's reflective thinking model proposed in 1910, whether they include all the steps he provided or some modification of them. Although in his book, *How We Think,* Dewey identified the steps most people use to solve problems, his steps have been followed as a way to organize problem-solving agendas for small groups (Schultz, 1996).

The problem-solving agenda presented here is a modified version of Dewey's model, with the addition of an orientation step at the beginning. The six steps are:

1. Check-in
2. Analyze the problem
3. Brainstorm solutions
4. Evaluate the better solutions
5. Reach consensus on the best solution
6. Implement the solution

Before we look at each step in detail, it's important to mention that the variations in the quality of decisions arrived at by groups can be accounted for by the ability of group members to perform four important decision-making functions. They are the effective assessment and discussion (1) of the problem, (2) the criteria for the solution, (3) the strengths of the proposed solutions, and (4) the weaknesses of the proposed solutions (Hirokawa, 1988). You will notice that these four functions are incorporated into the standard agenda we will now examine.

Step I: Check-In

The first step the group must take is to provide members with the opportunity to establish a supportive and trusting social dimension. Without a healthy social dimension, the group will not be able to function to maximum effectiveness.

Initially, the check-in period might require a substantial amount of time. Perhaps even the entire meeting. The check-in for the group encourages members to introduce themselves to one another by sharing any pertinent professional and personal information they feel may be helpful in letting other members know who they are. It can also be beneficial for members to share any previous experience, knowledge, or expertise they may have in the area, or related areas, to the problem they will be addressing.

After the group has established a supportive, friendly social dimension, the check-in step of each meeting becomes less involved. Usually, each member will take 30 to 60 seconds to share how things have been going in his or her life since the group last met. Much useful information can be provided during the group's check-in, and I've found these five minutes to be important to maintaining the group's social dimension.

Step 2:   Analyze the Problem

Analysis of the problem is the second step the group takes to solve a problem. Fruitful discussion during this stage of the process requires that group members have already researched the problem before coming to the meeting and are ready to share and discuss the following questions:

1. What is the problem?
2. What is the question of policy?
3. What is the nature of the problem?
4. Whom does the problem affect?
5. How serious is the problem?
6. What are causes of the problem?
7. What solutions have been attempted before?
8. What will happen if the problem is not solved?
9. What are the constraints for a workable solution?
10. What are three possible solutions that satisfy your criteria?

These 10 questions for problem analysis are not the only ones that can be considered when investigating a problem. They happen to be the most frequently asked questions of problem-solving groups I have worked with in the past. *Feel free to modify, delete, and add to this list as you and your group sees fit.* We will spend a considerable amount of time in the next chapter discussing how to research these questions. But for now, all I want to say is that the quality of your group's research will determine the quality of the information for the remainder of the group's activities.

Step 3:   Brainstorm Solutions

The primary purpose in the brainstorming step is to generate a large number of ideas without evaluation. The most serious threat to a group's attempt to select a workable and acceptable solution to any problem is the group's inability to generate more than two or three solutions to solve the problem.

I believe a group should never stop brainstorming until it has generated at least 30 possible solutions—not two or three, but 30!

During the brainstorming process, each group member writes down every suggestion made during the session (including his or her own suggestions). Number each suggestion as the group moves from item to item. The primary rule is that no evaluation of any idea during this stage of the problem-solving process is permitted. Members sit in a circle and contribute possible solutions to the problem under study. There is no rationale, explanation, or justification for each suggestion, simply the suggestion. Assign a number to it. Then go to the next suggestion until you reach at least 30 suggestions! Here are some guidelines for a successful brainstorming session:

1. Devote a specific period of time to brainstorming.
2. Every member must take notes, numbering each item.
3. No evaluation of any idea is permitted.
4. No questions, storytelling, explanations, or tangential talking is permitted.
5. Quantity of ideas, not quality, is desired.
6. The wilder the ideas the better.
7. Combine ideas.

You will discover some group members will enjoy this process of generating ideas without evaluation. It's not what we're accustomed to in our daily lives. There is often so much evaluation, judgment, and criticism of everything we think, feel, say, and do that a period of no evaluation is a welcomed experience. Enjoy it!

Step 4:   Evaluate the Better Solutions

Now's the time to slip back into a more critical thinking frame of mind.

Before you actually evaluate the better solutions against the criteria you've established in the second step, you need to spend some time throwing out the ridiculous, illegal, and impractical suggestions created during the brainstorming session. This is where the numbers come in handy. Instead of reading the entire proposal or idea you want to discard or throw out, you simply announce the number to the group. If they agree, they'll tell you. If not, they'll tell you. Either way, using the number instead of reading off the entire suggestion or idea each time will save you time, energy, and effort.

Once the group has 10 to 15 ideas or solutions worth examining, then the real task of step four begins—discussion of the strengths and weaknesses of the better solutions on the list. Here are some guidelines for a more effective discussion:

1. Discuss one solution at a time.
2. Consider both its strengths and weaknesses.
3. Consider how many constraints each solution satisfies.
4. Move to another solution quickly. Don't get stuck.
5. Avoid lumping solutions into one large conglomeration.
6. Don't be afraid to challenge a solution. Now's the time to share your reservations.

Evaluation of the better solutions will take time. Keep the six guidelines in mind when considering the better solutions. Speak your mind. Now's the time to voice your reservations as well as your preferences. Above all, listen for understanding while other members are sharing their reservations and preferences.

Step 5: Reach Consensus on the Best Solution

As the group discusses the better solutions, two or possibly three solutions will keep surfacing during the discussion. When you notice this occurring, mention it to the group. Let them know the group may be arriving at some agreement or common ground.

As the group narrows the selection to two or three, begin to look for areas of agreement within the group. Try to discover any common ground contained in the remaining solutions. Bring these to the attention of the group.

A second mini-brainstorming session may be appropriate at this time to generate a few related solutions to the two or three remaining in hopes of discovering one solution that is workable and acceptable to all group members. Remember, for consensus to occur, everyone must find the solution workable and acceptable.

To test for consensus, ask group members if they can live with this particular solution. They might object, stating it's not their first choice or they're not overly pleased with the solution. Just smile and repeat the question that tests for consensus: "But can you live with this solution for a period of time?"

After the group has reached consensus on a solution, take a break and celebrate. Remember the reinforcement phase of group development? Call out for pizza and soft drinks. The group deserves it!

Step 6: Implement the Solution

After you've cleaned up the pizza crumbs and empty soft drink cans, the group needs to implement the solution, which involves three steps—planning a timetable, assigning implementation tasks, and evaluating the implementation process. If the group is not required to implement the solution, this final step can be disregarded.

Plan a timetable. The group needs to divide the implementation of the solution into its component objectives and assign dates for the completion of those objectives. Be as specific as possible when you describe the component objectives.

Assign tasks. Assign individual members to complete the various tasks. Make certain each member knows the task and the date by which the task must be accomplished. Everyone should have the phone numbers of all group members, because communication is critical to the success of the project at this stage.

Evaluate implementation. The evaluation of the group's effectiveness in implementing the solution to the problem can be accomplished during a face-to-face meeting or over the telephone. Changes in procedure or approach might need to be made for future groups. Additional resources might need to be secured. And individual members might need to be encouraged, pushed, or congratulated. If the implementation was a success and all members are satisfied with their performance and that of the group, once again, I would suggest a social get-together to celebrate a job well done.

Reanalyze the problem (if necessary). If the solution fails to meet the group's expectations or standards, members might need to return to the beginning of the standard agenda and reanalyze the problem in Step 2. The evaluation of the implementation might have provided valuable information or a new perspective that was not initially available to the group. Many times, it's only after a solution is implemented that incomplete, inaccurate, or faulty analysis of the problem becomes apparent. In any case, the group can return to Step 2 and begin the entire process again.

THE CIRCULAR NATURE OF PROBLEM-SOLVING

The standard agenda provides groups with the most complete and time-tested problem-solving method (Wood et al., 1986), but that does not mean groups necessarily follow a linear, step-by-step process when they solve problems in the real world. That's why I include the *reanalysis of the problem* in Step 6 (as described in the previous paragraph). It enables a group to return full circle to the beginning of the agenda and begin the process again with additional information and new insight.

This circular approach to problem-solving is supported by the research of Marshall Poole (1981), who discovered that 23 percent of the decisions in problem-solving groups resulted from a strictly linear, decision-making sequence of phases, while approximately 47 percent of the decisions were made in repeated cycles of focusing on the problem, then the solution, then back to the problem. Finally, 30 percent of the decisions were made by the groups focusing their discussion only on solutions with little or no attention given to the analysis of the problem.

These findings are helpful when you use the standard agenda because they serve as a reminder that group problem-solving is not always a linear, step-by-step process, but more often is circular and dynamic, not following clear-cut divisions. Your group might begin with the analysis of the problem, then skip to a discussion of a solution, and return to problem analysis. Or, as I mentioned earlier, the group might actually implement a solution, only to discover that they need to return to the beginning of the agenda and begin again with additional information and insight. Don't get upset when these things occur. That's simply the circular nature of problem-solving.

Don't take this, however, as license to disregard the standard agenda and engage in a nonstructured approach to solving problems. Research repeatedly reminds us that a systematic approach to solving problems will help increase a group's effectiveness in the analysis of the problem, generation of possible solutions, and decision quality (Hirokawa, 1985; Gouran, 1991). Your goal is to give the group the flexibility to engage in a dynamic, circular decision-making process, within a systematic approach to solving problems.

The standard agenda will provide you and your group with a time-tested systematic approach to problem-solving. The group's flexibility in its application will ensure that group members will be given the freedom to do their best work.

Every problem you face provides the opportunity for you to do your best.

This chapter examined the myths of small group problem-solving, decision-making techniques, discussion questions, the standard problem-solving agenda, and the circular nature of problem-solving itself. Groups achieve the highest-quality decisions when they are knowledgeable, structured in their problem-solving, and engaged in a flexible, dynamic discussion process within that structure.

INDIVIDUAL AND GROUP EXERCISES

Exercise 5.1   Analyzing a Personal Problem

The beauty of the problem-solving agenda is its applicability to your personal life as well as to groups. Examine a problem or conflict you are currently experiencing (or have experienced) in your personal life. It doesn't matter whether it's a relationship problem, an employment issue, or a living situation. After you've identified a specific problem from your personal life, complete the following questions:

1. Describe in one sentence what specifically is the problem.

_____

2. Whom does the problem affect?

_____

3. How serious is the problem? Circle the appropriate conditions:

  I think about it occasionally.   It affects my relationships with others.

  I think about it often.   It affects my job/school performance.

  I obsess about the problem.   It affects my daily functioning.

4. What are some causes of the problem?

_____

_____

5. What solutions have you already attempted to solve this problem?

_____

_____

6. What do you think will happen if the problem is not solved?

_____

_____

7. What are some constraints to a workable solution?

_____

What did you think about this exercise? Were you honest in your answers to the questions? Were you able to answer all the questions or were there some questions you weren't able to respond to? Does this exercise change or modify how you see your problem? For the better? For the worse?

Exercise 5.2   Brainstorming Solutions to the Problem

Now that you've analyzed this problem of yours, try to brainstorm five possible solutions. I know you've been over this a million times, but most likely you've proposed the same two or three solutions over and over. This time, get crazy. Brainstorm some wild and ridiculous ideas! Give yourself two minutes for this exercise. Here goes! List at least five possible solutions to this problem of yours (I'll supply the other five).

1. _____

2. _____

3. _____

4. _____

5. _____

6. Don't do anything for one year and see what happens.

7. Make the current situation worse by increasing the symptoms.

8. See the problem as an invitation to become a different kind of person.

9. Leave the situation / the state / the country.

10. Lose interest in the problem by creating a more serious problem in your life.

How did the brainstorming session go? Did you refrain from evaluating your solutions? Could you get a little wild and crazy in your suggestions? How did that feel to you? What do you think of your list? What do you think of the five solutions I suggested at the end?

Exercise 5.3   Group Problem-Solving Activity

Have your group attempt to proceed through the first three steps of the problem-solving agenda presented in this chapter on a "small," manageable problem facing the group. Don't select a big problem, just a small problem so group members can get a feel for this approach to orientation, problem analysis, and brainstorming. Make sure each group member has a list of the questions in Step 2 and receives instruction on the brainstorming technique. Good luck!

SIX

PREPARING FOR DISCUSSION

**The secret to success is to know something
that everyone else doesn't.
–Henry Ford**

There's a story about a high-rise apartment owner who tried to get his broken furnace to work after it quit for the second time that winter. The owner hired three different furnace technicians to locate the problem. But each time the problem could not be solved. His shivering, disgruntled apartment tenants threatened to sue him for breach of contract.

Finally, the owner phoned a fourth technician, who listened to his problem. The old technician guaranteed he could solve the problem.

"Are you sure?" demanded the young apartment owner.

"I think I've seen this problem before," assured the technician. "Most mechanics wouldn't know where to look, but I'm certain I can help you."

Later that day, the mechanic met the owner at the apartment high-rise and the old man asked to see the basement where the furnace was located. The old furnace was a complicated, confusing maze of pipes, wires, and odd-shaped contraptions. This same scene had stumped the three previous technicians, who were not accustomed to such a labyrinth of metal, dials, and piping.

The old man walked deeper into this jungle of sheet metal and piping, his flashlight sweeping small arcs of yellow light into the confusion, as the owner followed blindly behind. Eventually, the mechanic stopped, felt the metal above his head, then selected a rubber hammer from his tool pouch. He gently tapped once on a small cylindrical box located above one of the thermostats.

Immediately, the giant heater grunted twice, then coughed up a deep roar of massive flames within the once-dark interior of the furnace. The fans began to swirl, pushing the heat up into the building. Within a minute, cheers could be heard from the tenants on the lowest floors, as the warm air flowed for the first time in four days.

"You're a genius!" shouted the young apartment owner. "What will this minor miracle cost me?"

"The bill is $500," replied the mechanic.

"That's outrageous! You're charging me $500 for tapping a metal box just one time?" he screamed.

"Oh, no. The tap of my hammer was only $1," smiled the old man. "Knowing where to tap cost you $499."

This chapter will examine ways to increase and use your knowledge about a specific topic. We will explore where to research, what to research, how to construct an information sheet, and suggest methods to test evidence and reasoning. Before we do, let's discuss our need to increase our knowledge.

YOU DON'T KNOW EVERYTHING

The meaning of this section title is obvious—we don't know everything. If we did, we wouldn't need the help of others to solve problems in the real world. But we don't know everything.

The furnace technician knew how to fix the furnace, but he might not know how to balance the books. The apartment owner might know how to balance the books, but he didn't know how to fix the furnace. In fact, the first three mechanics didn't know how to locate the problem. Each person knows some things, but not everything about everything. You don't, and I don't.

Yet people like you and me will participate in a problem-solving group without ever once researching the problem, interviewing experts in the field, or even giving the issue any prior consideration or thought before taking our seat at the meeting.

Many times, we simply show up at the meeting, glance at the material sent to us by the chairperson, grab a cup of coffee, and settle down in our chair for another long discussion. I know this happens often. I've been guilty of it more than I'd care to admit.

Our lack of preparation is a result of many factors. First, we're too busy with other matters to devote any time to research. Second, we might never have learned how to conduct library research or interview an expert. Finally, many of us don't prepare for a problem-solving discussion because of laziness. A million other things seem more appealing, like skiing, shopping, visiting, eating, gossiping, and sleeping. Even staring at the walls of our office with our feet on the desk would be better than researching.

WE CAN ALWAYS KNOW MORE

Ideally, a problem-solving group would be made up of individuals who are experts in the problem area they are examining. Yet, that is not practical. The majority of problem-solving groups are made up of interested and concerned people like you and me. We want to get a candidate elected. We want to put a stop sign at the end of our street. We want to raise funds for a favorite charity. Or we might just want to make our neighborhoods safer from crime.

No matter what we're trying to accomplish as a group, research can help us in our attempt to achieve the best solution for our problem. You won't necessarily have to make a trip to the city library, but you could phone around to see what other cities have done to reduce crime in their neighborhoods. You might conduct a series of brief interviews with a police officer, a Neighborhood Watch coordinator, a locksmith, and even an ex-thief to collect information and ideas that will benefit your group's attempts to make your neighborhood safer from crime.

Research is not only looking up information in your local library. It's any activity that broadens or increases your information base on any topic or subject. In fact, some of your most helpful information will come from experts who deal with your group's problem every day of their lives.

No matter how much you know about the specific problem or issue confronting your group, you can always know more. I believe the more information and evidence a group has at its disposal, the greater the probability its efforts will produce a solution that is workable and acceptable to all group members.

WHERE TO RESEARCH

The four primary sources for information about your group's topics are your own knowledge and experience, library research, interviews, and surveys.

Tapping Your Personal Knowledge and Experience

One of the most neglected areas of research is your own knowledge of and experience in the problem. Take a moment to sit in a quiet part of your house and close your eyes. Imagine a scene from the problem your group is researching. In the case of bicycle theft, what experiences have you had in this area? Has a bicycle of yours ever been stolen? Have your neighbors, friends, or relatives had their bikes stolen? What did you/they experience? What did you/they learn? What precautions do you/they currently take to reduce the chances of future theft? Do any books, television documentaries, magazine articles, or lectures related to this topic come to mind? Do any people having special expertise or interest in this topic come to mind?

As you reflect on your own experience and knowledge of the problem, keep notes with pencil and paper. Jot down any idea, thought, experience, or feeling that may provide information to the group's discussion. You'll be surprised by the amount of knowledge and experience you might already possess about the problem.

This activity of surveying your own knowledge and experience can also generate ideas on where to look for information and whom to seek for expert testimony. Let your mind wander as you research your own experience. Keep your mind open to discovering forgotten experiences and bits of information in the corners of your mind.

Using Library Resources

Any library, regardless of size, usually provides the following sources of information that you will need to research your topic.

The card catalog indexes all the library's books by author, title, and subject. This catalog is your primary guide to the books in the library. If you are unfamiliar with its operation, ask for assistance.

Periodicals (magazines, journals, and newspapers) are another source of information for your research efforts. The *Reader's Guide to Periodical Literature* will be your most valuable resource for locating periodical articles related to your topic. Periodical information is generally more current than information provided by books and encyclopedias. The *Reader's Guide* indexes the articles of more than 130 American periodicals on a wide range of topics.

Your library should have your local daily *newspaper indexes* in addition to the *New York Times Index*. Local newspapers will often provide the most valuable information concerning problems specific to your area. (You might also consider contacting the local newspaper and explaining your research project. Newspaper folks are often helpful in assisting you in anyway they can.)

Most libraries utilize computer technology to make your research easier, faster, and more comprehensive. *On-line computers* speed up your survey of books and periodicals. The *Internet* provides you with information sources from all around the globe. And *CD-ROM technology* gives you access to vast quantities of information available from encyclopedias, periodicals, and newspaper indexes. If you are already familiar with computers, you know the speed, power, and enjoyment this technology provides. If you are not, don't be afraid to ask the librarian for some basic instruction on their use. A few minutes of computer instruction will open up a new world of information to you.

Conducting Interviews

Although you may be reluctant to ask for an interview from a local expert, the rewards of doing so can go beyond that of gaining valuable information. Many a friendship, both professional and personal, and many a job have blossomed because of a 15-minute interview. Not only will you be gathering expert opinion regarding your topic of discussion, you will be given the opportunity to connect with another human being you would have otherwise been a stranger to.

The first step in conducting an interview is to decide with *whom* you want to talk. If your problem is neighborhood crime, you might want to speak with the local police chief. If your topic deals with electing a local candidate, you might want to talk with a political campaign director.

After you decide on one or two experts to interview, the second step is to *request* an interview. Whether you request an interview in person, over the telephone, or in a formal letter, keep your request brief and friendly. Let the person know you would like to spend only 15 minutes interviewing him at his convenience (not yours). If he cannot grant an interview, thank him for his time and try the next candidate. If he agrees to the interview, great!

The third step is to write a list of *questions* for the interview itself. This should be done only *after* you have researched the topic from your own knowledge and experience and in the library. This preparation will enable you to ask more enlightened, specific, and articulate questions.

The fourth step is the *interview* itself. Be punctual. Nothing is more annoying to your interviewee than your arriving late to a meeting you requested. Dress up for the interview. Don't arrive in your t-shirt and old jeans. And stick to your time limit of 15 minutes. At the end, thank the interviewee.

Finally, after you've returned from the interview, take a moment to write a brief *thank you card or letter* to the interviewee. The few minutes and the cost of the stamp will add a touch of class that few interviewers ever consider.

Taking Surveys

For some problem-solving topics, the attitudes and opinions of a group of individuals might provide valuable information and help in your decision-making efforts. A survey can gather information about the seriousness and nature of the problem, generate a list of potential solutions, or provide you with an idea of the support or opposition your solution will receive if proposed. These and many other uses suggest that surveys are a rich source of information for your group.

Whether it's randomly surveying 20 employees concerning their feelings on reducing medical coverage rather than cutting wages, or polling the neighbors on their feelings about lowering the speed limit in the neighborhood, the opinions of a group of people can be extremely informative.

If you decide to include a survey in your research, keep these five suggestions in mind. First, develop a clear idea of what you are trying to achieve in your survey. Second, select a large enough population to be representative of the entire population being sampled. In some cases, the number of people affected by the problem is small so that all of them can be polled. Third, decide whether to interview people face-to-face, over the phone, or by mail. Fourth, construct a questionnaire that is to the point, clearly written, and asks only what needs to be addressed. And finally, test the clarity of your survey in a pilot study or mini-survey.

For most problem-solving efforts, your survey doesn't need to be too elaborate or statistically perfect. A simple polling of neighbor's attitudes or the collection of coworker's opinions will be adequate. If a more complicated or involved survey is necessary, you may want to consult a book on survey methods or ask someone who has had previous experience in conducting surveys.

WHAT TO RESEARCH

Now that you know four areas to research for your problem, we need to consider what you should be researching or looking for. The items you want to seek information and evidence about are the questions from Step 2 of your standard agenda—analyzing the problem.

These questions focus on your research efforts. You should try to gather as much information as you can regarding these questions. These are merely suggestions. Feel free to add, modify, and delete from this list as you see fit.

1. What Is the Problem?

The group should agree on what the problem is and define it. Avoid vague, general descriptions of the problem. Be as specific as possible. Instead of "crime," your group might want to focus more specifically on "department store shoplifting by pre-teenage children in the Santa Clara County." This definition will focus the group's research and discussion much more than a general description.

2. What Is the Question of Policy?

The group should agree on the question of policy before you begin researching the topic. Remember to begin the question of policy with "What should be done about...?"

3. What Is the Nature of the Problem?

Find information describing the specific nature of the problem you are investigating. What exactly is the problem? What are the parameters of the problem? Are there any limitations or special conditions presented by the problem? How long has the problem existed? What is the history of the problem?

4. Whom Does the Problem Affect?

The fourth question you need to research is who is affected by the problem. Does the problem affect primarily men, women, or children? Young or old people ? Does the problem affect a specific subgroup? Try to get as much information about those affected by the problem as possible.

5. How Serious Is the Problem?

This is a question of value. Not all individuals will perceive the problem as being serious, but you need to establish some measurement of its magnitude, scope, and significance. Try to obtain statistical information describing the size and seriousness of the problem. Expert testimony on its seriousness is also helpful in determining how the group should address the problem.

6. What Causes the Problem?

This can be both a question of fact and a question of value. It's a question of value because experts may hold differing beliefs on the probable cause or causes of the problem. Your task is to obtain information on the problem's original cause or causes. Get as much information as possible, citing how and why the problem came into existence.

7. What Solutions Were Tried Already?

In your research, be on the lookout for solutions that have been attempted already to reduce or eliminate the current problem. Be as specific as possible when you describe solutions that have been previously attempted. Also list organizations and individuals who attempted a solution. Describe the effectiveness of their attempt(s) and discuss any suggestions the organizations and individuals may have for future attempts.

8. What Will Happen if the Problem Isn't Solved?

What do experts or the literature say will happen if this problem is not solved? Once again, this is primarily a question of value, because experts will have differing views. Describe as specifically as you can the situation or conditions that will result if the problem is not solved or its effects reduced.

9. What Are the Constraints for a Workable Solution?

Suggest at least three specific constraints for a workable solution to this problem. For instance, three criteria for a solution to the problem of reducing neighborhood theft may be that the solution must (1) costs less than $500 to implement, (2) be implemented within 60 days, and (3) involve participation by all residents. These constraints will help determine the merit of the solutions the group considers.

10. What Are Three Solutions That Satisfy Your Criteria?

After you have completed researching the problem (questions 3 through 9), brainstorm three solutions. You might want to brainstorm more, but try to keep it manageable. You will be sharing your ideas during the group's brainstorming session.

CONSTRUCTING AN INFORMATION SHEET

An easy method for recording all your research data is to use an *information sheet*, which contains the 10 questions from your problem analysis and the evidence you gathered for each question. You should cite the author, source, and date for each piece of information you include, in case another group member questions your data. For an interview, cite the expert's name, qualifications, and date of the interview. Here's an example of a question and the corresponding evidence and documentation for an information sheet.

6. What are the causes of the problem?
   A. "Increased drug use is the primary cause of increased home robberies."
      Police Chief Mark Henson, San Rafael Police. Interview, 8/26/96.
   B. "The increase in home robberies is due to the increase in drug use."
      Article by Sheila Graves, *San Rafael Times*, 8/18/96.

When you research the answers to the questions in Step 2 of the standard agenda, you may need to refer to more than one kind of research source. Don't limit yourself to only magazines, newspapers, books, or expert opinions. Use as many sources of information as you can discover.

TESTING EVIDENCE AND REASONING

The purpose of researching the problem is to broaden the information base available to your group. Each piece of information or evidence added to the discussion increases the group's chances of discovering a workable and acceptable solution to the problem. Without the research of each group member, the probability of discovering a viable solution is decreased. Information is power.

During the group's problem-solving discussions, members share information, especially during Step 2 (analysis of the problem) and Step 4 (discussion of the strengths and weaknesses of the better solutions). It is for the benefit of the group that members carefully examine the evidence, proposals, and the reasoning supporting the proposals. Without careful examination and testing of the evidence and reasoning, the effectiveness of the group's decision-making and problem-solving will be compromised. Only with careful scrutiny of both evidence and reasoning can the group select viable solutions.

Three categories of research contributions require examination—opinions, evidence, and proposals. These are the three most prevalent contributions of researched information to group discussion. We will now examine what each category is and how to evaluate it.

Testing Opinions

Although personal opinions of group members are not technically a documented piece of information or evidence, they can often be presented as such without the expert testimony or evidence to support it. Examples of personal opinions are:

> The rise in crime is due to the influx of minorities into our area.
> Juveniles are the cause of the increase in crime.
> The solution is more state and federal laws against drug addiction.

In each example, the personal opinion was stated not as an I-statement, but rather as a statement of fact or expert testimony. When you hear statements such as these in a discussion, you can force the speaker to own his statements simply by asking, *"Is this your personal opinion?"* Most of the time, the speaker will qualify his personal opinion by rephrasing his opinion, such as:

> *I think* the rise in crime is due to the influx of minorities into our area.
> *It's my opinion* that juveniles are the cause of the increase in crime.
> *I believe* the solution is more state and federal laws against drug addiction.

The importance of forcing I-statements is that the speaker cannot subtly persuade or influence the group with more credibility than his own opinion should carry. It also separates personal opinion from expert opinion during discussion. If the speaker doesn't own his opinion, but instead says, "It's my opinion and the opinion of others," or "Experts say the same thing," then ask, *"What evidence do you have to support your last statement?"* The purpose of asking for evidence is to examine the support for the speaker's statements.

The sharing of opinions is important to group discussion. With them, the group gets a feel for the attitudes and positions of each member. However, opinions need to be posed as I-statements. If members don't own their opinions, their statements can be mistaken for expert testimony or research findings, which can lend unwarranted weight to their statements.

Testing Evidence

In the course of discussion, especially during problem analysis, group members may present documented evidence. Most of the time, you'll jot down the information in your notes if you think it's important, thereby adding to the group's information base. But on some occasions a piece of evidence might sound contradictory to the rest of the information presented on the problem. Or the evidence might sound old, or not as recent as you would like. Or you might want to know more about the author of the research, the publication, or source. If this is the case, then testing evidence is required. Testing the quantity, quality, recency, and relevancy of research presented during discussion is not only your right as a group member, it is also your responsibility. Let's briefly examine the four tests of evidence.

1. Testing quantity.   The evidence or information a group member presents may be documented fully, with author, source, and date, but you may want to know if there is other supporting evidence. To base decisions solely on one study or one expert testimony may not be the wisest course of action. Other experts who agree with the testimony or research presented lend additional strength to the position. You can test for the quantity of evidence by asking such questions as, Do you have *additional evidence* to support this point? Were there any *other studies* suggesting the same conclusion? Did anyone else find *similar evidence?* By asking for supporting evidence, you also encourage low-verbal group members to contribute.

2. Testing quality.   Group members might present reams of evidence supporting a certain point or position, but the quality of the sources or the qualifications of the authors or experts could be questionable. The second test of evidence is quality. You might need to know the source of the evidence, the qualifications of the author, or the specifics of the design of an experiment.

To test for the quality of evidence, the following questions can be helpful: *What* is the source of your evidence? *Where* did you find that information? *Who* is the author of your evidence? *Describe* the qualifications of the author. These and other related questions can test the quality of the evidence presented during discussion. Don't be afraid to ask questions about the quality of evidence. Most people will readily provide the additional information you are seeking. And an unwillingness to do so is also valuable information for the group to consider.

3. Testing recency.   The more recent the evidence, the more valuable it can be to the group. Outdated or old evidence or information provides questionable value to the discussion. If a member cannot cite the date of an article or research finding, the evidence

can be misleading or counterproductive if more recent and contradictory information has been discovered. That's why it's important to
know the recency of evidence shared in discussion. Here are some
questions that test for recency: *When* was that evidence published?
How recent is your information? *When* was the interview conducted?

4. Testing relevancy.   Evidence that is irrelevant to the discussion provides no valuable contribution to the discussion. The truth
or falsity of irrelevant evidence doesn't concern the group, for it has
no bearing on the topic being discussed. Often, irrelevant evidence
or information isn't identified as such during discussion and the discussion gets sidetracked and often derailed. Silent group members
who are reluctant to challenge the relevancy of such information
might feel frustration and hostility. For the sake of the task and social
dimensions of the group, you need to test the relevancy of evidence
by questioning its bearing on the topic. Here are some ways to pose
the question: *How* does your evidence *relate* to our discussion? *What's
the connection* between your evidence and the topic? *What is the
relevance* of your evidence to our discussion?

The four tests of evidence will improve the quality of group discussion. Without adequately testing questionable or unclear evidence,
the information being considered can be confusing, misleading, and
even harmful to the effectiveness and productivity of the discussion.

When testing evidence, keep these four guidelines in mind. First,
the purpose of testing information is clarification and thoughtful consideration, not personal attack or assault. Second, your nonverbal
communication cues should match this intent of clarification. Be soft
in your tone of voice. If the speaker is offended by your question
and responds defensively, maintain your gentle nonverbal posture.
Third, let the other person "save face." By this I mean give the person you are questioning some room to clarify, modify, or withdraw
his information. Don't push the speaker. Don't attack the speaker.
Simply pose your question and let him respond. Finally, submit your
own evidence to the four tests before you enter the discussion.

Testing Proposals

The testing of proposals occurs when the group discusses the
strengths and weaknesses of the better solutions.

A proposal is stated in the form of a solution to the problem the
group is considering. During the course of group discussion, many
proposals will be presented for consideration. Effective group prob-

lem-solving requires critical testing of these proposals. *Critical thinking* is the ability to reach a sound conclusion by making valid inferences from premises.

A *conclusion* is any proposal or claim the group is asked to believe or accept. The *premise* of a conclusion is any reason given to support its acceptance. An *inference* connects or links a particular premise to a conclusion. These inferences can be either valid or invalid. The logical structure of any argument would look like this:

Because (premise) and (premise), therefore, (conclusion).

For the purposes of group discussion, however, we will use the terms *proposal, reason,* and *inference* to test the ideas presented. Here's the logical structure using these terms:

Because (reason) and (reason), therefore, (proposal).

Here is an example of a proposal you might encounter in your group's problem-solving discussions:

We should adopt a salary freeze if profits drop by 10 percent *(proposal)*
because it has been successful in other companies *(reason)*
and it involves the participation of all employees *(reason)*.

Or stated in logical structure form:

Because it has been successful in other companies *(reason),* and
because it involves the participation of all employees *(reason),* we should
therefore adopt a salary freeze if profits drop by 10 percent *(proposal)*.

Very rarely will a proposal be stated with all its reasons. Usually someone will say, "I think we should freeze salaries if profits drop by 10 percent."

At this point in the discussion it's important to test the reasons supporting a particular proposal. The way you test is to ask for the reason or reasons supporting the proposal—"Let's examine the reasons supporting this solution." The inferences that link the reasons to the proposal are rarely stated; they are usually implied or suggested. Therefore, it is important to examine and test the validity of these inferences.

Inferences are either deductive or inductive. A *deductive inference* is one whose conclusion follows with logical necessity from the premises or reasons. If the premises or reasons are true, the conclusion must be true. For example:

Because all prison inmates must be at least 18 years old *(reason),*
and Bob is a prison inmate *(reason),*
therefore, Bob is at least 18 years old *(proposal).*

A deductive inference forces us to accept the conclusion. If the premises are true, there is no chance of the conclusion being false.

An *inductive inference,* on the other hand, is one where we project a likely or probable outcome or conclusion based on one or more known facts or experiences. The inductive inference does not force or guarantee the truth of the conclusion, it merely speaks to the probability of it being true. For example:

Because Bob has already served his prison term *(reason),*
and Bob has obeyed all the regulations of his probation *(reason),*
and Bob has been attending church regularly *(reason),*
therefore, Bob will never commit a crime again *(proposal).*

The important thing to remember about inductive inferences is that they cannot guarantee 100 percent the conclusion they suggest. They can suggest only a high probability of correctness or truth. In the example above, we cannot be 100 percent certain Bob will never commit a crime again, even though he served his time, obeyed the probation rules, and attends church.

Most inferences suggested in your group discussions will be inductive. In other words, you must test the validity and soundness of the reasons supporting each proposal. Here are some questions you can ask when testing inductive inferences:

Are there *sufficient* reasons to accept the proposal?
Are the reasons *directly relevant* to the proposal?
Do we have *sufficient evidence* to support each reason?
Is the *evidence* supporting each reason *acceptable, recent,* and *relevant?*

RECOGNIZING LOGICAL FALLACIES

In addition to testing the reasons supporting a proposal, you should be alert to any logical fallacies contained in the inferences suggested by each proposal. A *logical fallacy* is a mistake in logic or a mistaken or false belief. Here are five of the most common logical fallacies you will encounter in your discussions:

1. Overgeneralizing

An *overgeneralization* is a conclusion based on insufficient evidence. For instance, if there are two reports of car stereo thefts in your neighborhood during the past month, you might conclude that the rate of car stereo thefts is on the increase nationwide. This conclusion is not supported by the data. Two reports of car stereo thefts in your neighborhood is insufficient evidence to make generalizations about the nation. When this happens in a group, you should inquire about additional evidence to support the conclusion or suggest that there is insufficient evidence to support the claim.

2. Causal Fallacy

A causal fallacy is an argument that suggests two events are causally connected, though no such relationship is established. This is one of the most common fallacies made in discussion. Someone says, "We've never had a problem with car stereo thefts until you moved into the neighborhood." The speaker has assumed that the presence of the new neighbor is the cause of the problem, which may or may not be true. But a causal link has not been established. The speaker has provided no evidence showing the new neighbor is the cause of the problem.

If a causal fallacy is made, one approach you can take is to suggest additional causes or causal relationships that may explain the event. You can also mention that simply because these two events occur at the same time, it doesn't necessarily follow that one causes the other.

3. False Analogy

A false analogy assumes that because two things are alike in one or more respects, they are necessarily alike in some other respect. In group discussion, a solution to a problem is suggested because that solution worked somewhere else. Let's say someone draws the analogy between eating and marriage. Eating the same food day after day would quickly become boring, he argues. Therefore variety in food selection is desirable. Similarly, he concludes, having only one girlfriend can also become boring, so maintaining relationships with three women at the same time would eliminate such boredom.

Do you see the fallacy of this analogy? What works under one circumstance does not always work under another. If you believe a false analogy is being used, question the strength of the similarities of the two circumstances or situations. After careful examination, are you convinced the two situations are similar enough to warrant comparison?

4. Either–Or Thinking

This fallacy supposes that only two options are available for consideration and that one of them must be accepted by the group. "Either we do it this way or we do it that way." "Either you support the solution or you don't." "Either you are with the group or against the group." Each statement gives only two positions for consideration, when in reality, many positions are possible.

When either-or thinking happens, don't let your group be fooled into believing they can take or consider only two positions. There are always more. Challenge either-or thinking in your group by suggesting other options. Or speak in terms of more and less. For instance, instead of describing a proposal as good or bad, you can point out it is less expensive than some and more practical than others. Don't let the group's thinking become too rigid or limited.

5. Ad Hominem Argument (Attacking the Person)

This fallacy consists of attacking the opponent in a personal way as a means of ignoring or discrediting her evidence or position, instead of focusing debate on the evidence or issue under examination. The attack is leveled against the person's character, beliefs, or behavior as a means of diverting attention from the strength of her arguments and reasoning. When this occurs in a group, try to direct the discussion back to the issue or bring the attacker's behavior to the attention of the group.

This chapter explored ways to increase and use your knowledge about a specific topic. We discussed where to research, what to research, how to construct an information sheet, and suggested methods to test evidence and reasoning. When you work in groups, your knowledge base and ability to critically examine the information and reasoning employed by the group will determine the quality of your decisions.

INDIVIDUAL AND GROUP EXERCISES

Exercise 6.1   Personal Research Problem

Select one issue from your personal life that has been a cause of anxiety, frustration, anger, or worry. Be as specific as possible in your description of the issue. Next, select one person, either living or dead, you would want to interview to provide insight into the issue. This person could be a religious figure, a famous scientist, a deceased family member, or anyone else you believe could provide information or expertise. Finally, write three questions you want answered during your 15-minute interview. The person will answer each of your questions. Construct your questions carefully so the person can provide the most information to your inquiries.

Describe your personal issue. I am concerned about _____

_____

Whom are you going to interview? _____

List three questions this person will answer.

1. _____

2. _____

3. _____

Whom did you select for your interview? Why did you select this person? How do you feel about the questions you asked? What do your questions tell you about how you see this issue? What would you do if this person did in fact answer your three questions? Would you change your thinking, feeling, or behavior concerning your issue? If this issue is not resolved to your satisfaction, what will that be like for you? What have you discovered about yourself in this exercise?

Exercise 6.2   Group Research

Have your group select one communication behavior that all group members feel they should improve. Listening, clarifying messages, summarizing ideas, resolving conflicts, and encouraging low-verbal members to contribute are some examples of these behaviors. Once a topic is selected, have each member independently research two library resources and interview one expert in an effort to gather information about this particular communication behavior. Meet as a group and share your research.

S E V E N
GUIDING DISCUSSION

**If you don't know where you're going
any road will do.
–Basho**

Hansen is a speck on the map about 30 miles southeast of Twin Falls, Idaho. My wife's uncle runs a cattle ranch just outside Hansen, right at the foot of the Sawtooth Mountains. Uncle Chuck's house is nestled in a sleepy little hollow, flanked on both sides by a year-round creek and shaded by a grove of willows.

Several years ago, my family and I spent four days at Uncle Chuck's. Time stands still at his ranch. It takes me two days just to unwind and slip into country time. Schedules there are governed by the rising and the setting of the sun. Folks there talk slow, with a deep richness, unhurried, and seemingly unaffected by this century. I like all this, up at Hansen.

But what I like best is watching Sheila and Ted, Uncle Chuck's two spirited border collies, keeping a hundred head of cattle moving straight on course during a cattle drive.

Border collies, I'm told, are the smartest cattle dogs in the world. A hundred cows can be packed into a tightly stuffed orb by one dog and moved almost effortlessly, like the shadow of a cloud rolling silently over the flowing landscape. The dogs dodge, dart, shove, and pack the cows into one obedient, single-minded mass of livestock, headed for a yet unseen destination.

One rancher down the road from Chuck's went into a three-month depression when his border collie, Nick, died of old age. The rancher shed more tears over Nick's death than he did when his wife left him. At least that's what Uncle Chuck says, and Uncle Chuck doesn't exaggerate. In fact, he doesn't say much at all. And that's why the last night we were in Hansen, Uncle Chuck surprised me with something he shared.

"Too bad our cattlemen's association didn't have some border collies to keep us in line," he lamented, as we sat on the back porch steps. "Seems like our association can't ever seem to agree on anything because we don't stick to the topic."

"Like those cows, maybe you need some help staying on track," I suggested.

"Yeah. And we might be dumber than cows. At least cows don't fight with one another," he smiled.

I smiled too as we listened to the water in the creek begin its journey to the sea.

This chapter will explore ways to keep group discussion not only on track, but focused on the most effective and productive path to effective decision-making. By utilizing task guiding behaviors, social guiding behaviors, and dysfunctional guiding behaviors, you will promote more successful discussion within your group.

WE EACH HAVE A SEPARATE PATH

The funny thing about trying to keep five or six people on track during a discussion is that it's not as easy as you might think. One person will start the discussion with one idea only to be interrupted by someone else, who begins to weave a second, unrelated thought or idea into the discussion, while two people chuckle at a humorous remark made by a third speaker. And the sixth member of the group is staring out the window, oblivious to the other three conversations.

Each person, it seems, has a different idea of where to go, what to do, and how to do it. Some members talk a lot; others don't. At times, each group member seems to be taking a separate path.

The initial task during any discussion is not solving a problem. That will come in its own time, if it is to come at all. The initial task of the group is to keep the discussion focused, coordinated, and on track in a supportive, open atmosphere. No matter how well informed, committed, and articulate each member might be, the group can wander aimlessly, like cattle without those border collies, if it cannot stay focused.

GUIDING DISCUSSION TO A SHARED PATH

This chapter will show you specific ways to guide the discussion of the group so it stays on track. Instead of members taking separate paths, you will be guiding discussion to a shared path.

Sort of like border-collie training, but with a higher calling in mind. You won't be as pushy and controlling as a border collie, but you will know the moves to keep the five or six of you on track during your discussions. Remember, this is the initial task of the group—to keep the group together and focused on what needs to be done. A collection of geniuses wandering off in separate directions, not coordinating and sharing their individual talents, is a waste indeed. Don't let this happen to your group.

The communication behaviors you will learn are called *guiding behaviors* because they keep the discussion on track and coordinate the participation and contributions of the individual members in the most productive manner possible.

You will learn three categories of guiding behaviors. First, *task guiding behaviors* are intended to keep the discussion productive, participatory, and on track. Second, *social guiding behaviors* are designed to establish and maintain healthy interpersonal relationships between group members. Finally, *dysfunctional guiding behaviors* are aimed at correcting disruptive or counterproductive behavior within the group.

EVERY GROUP MEMBER IS A LEADER

Although you can view each of these behaviors as a leadership task or role, I have intentionally separated them from Chapter 8, Leading a Group. The reason for this is that every group member should be skilled at guiding the discussion, not just the designated group leader.

If every group member is aware of and skilled in the use of these guiding behaviors, then the overall group performance will be enhanced. If knowledge and skills training is vested in only one individual (the leader) or two individuals within a group can often lead to an imbalance of power and thus decision-making. That's why each group member should develop these guiding behavior skills.

In some books these behaviors are referred to as roles. *Roles* can be defined as the expected behavior of a particular individual within the group. This perspective suggests that group members will specialize in one or more of the various task and social-maintenance roles that they feel comfortable and proficient in performing.

The roles approach, however, is limiting and confining. From this perspective, group members begin to look for their special "calling" or "talent," and concentrate on developing and implementing only those one or two roles during discussions. Sasha becomes the "information analyzer," Yoko the "harmonizer," Fred the "negotiator," Mohammed the "gate keeper," and Suzanne the "information provider."

Eventually, this behavior (or behaviors) becomes the "expected" function of that member, and the group will look to, and wait for, him or her to perform the behavior. It's called task or *role specialization*. Nice term, but group members possess greater influence and control of the discussion when each person isn't locked into one or two ways of behaving. *The goal is for each group member to discover a wide array of guiding behaviors he or she can put to use during a discussion, depending on the situation, the mood of the group, and his or her particular inclination at that given moment.*

The verb approach (guiding behaviors) provides a more empowering, dynamic way of looking at the process of group discussion, while the noun approach (roles) can unconsciously limit an individual's options and restrict performance. Each person in the group is capable and entitled to guide the discussion from time to time. You need to discover the leader within!

TASK GUIDING BEHAVIORS

Kenneth Benne and Paul Sheats have proposed a list of task and social roles that have enabled us to get a clearer idea of what specific behaviors individuals can perform in groups. The following is a modified list of their roles to help you understand the ways you can guide group discussion. Task guiding behaviors are those behaviors that initiate and maintain a productive task dimension during the group's discussions. The seven task guiding behaviors are requesting information, providing information, clarifying information, guiding discussion, summarizing, analyzing and reasoning, and negotiating.

Requesting Information

Requesting information from the group is an important function of every group member. It serves to broaden the information base of the group, initiate interaction when the discussion lulls, and encourage low-verbal members to contribute. Requesting information is a basic communication skill that invites others to communicate, participate, and contribute. Here are some examples of requesting information:

> What do we think about...? How do we feel about...? Does anyone have any information dealing with...? Does anyone have any evidence concerning...? Did anyone interview an expert about...? What information haven't we shared yet?

The important thing to remember about requesting information is that you are opening up the discussion to everyone again. This behavior can often have an invigorating effect on a discussion that is needlessly stuck on an overworked item. It can also serve to discourage a high-verbal member from monopolizing a discussion.

Providing Information

Sharing evidence, information, or personal opinion is a vital behavior each group member is expected to perform. Without the sharing of information, there can be no discussion. You have thought about and researched the topic before attending the meeting, so you are prepared to provide the group with the fruits of your labor. Here are some ways to begin:

> (Providing evidence/information)
> In my research I discovered... I read that... One study suggested...
> During my interview with _____ I learned that...
> According to... A recent poll concluded that...
>
> (Providing opinion)
> I think... It's my opinion that... I believe... I feel...
> It's my understanding that...

If you research the topic, you owe it to the group to share or provide as much relevant information to the discussion as possible. By withholding or failing to share your information, you can prevent the group from arriving at the wisest decisions and proposing the best solutions. You could be holding the one piece of information the group needs to succeed!

Clarifying Information

After a group member shares information, some confusion or question might arise about the content or meaning of the statement. This is when you need to clarify any ambiguous information. Here are some ways you can initiate that process:

> Are you saying...?   Do you mean...?   Do I understand your research to suggest that...?   So, this tells us that...?   Another way to say this may be...?   Can we interpret the evidence to suggest...?   Could you repeat it?

The purpose of clarifying information is to ensure that the picture in the speaker's head is the same as or similar to the one you intended. Clarify any ambiguous information presented to the group. Take the time to ask questions. This is true for group discussion work as well as for your personal life.

Guiding Discussion

Guiding-discussion behaviors keep the discussion on the agenda, regulate participation, and announce time limits. Without these behaviors the group loses direction. Notice how powerful each of these behaviors is in guiding the group:

> (Initiating the agenda)
> Let's define the problem....
> Can we move onto brainstorming solutions?
> I think we can move to the next step of....
>
> (Maintaining the agenda)
> I think we need to return to the agenda....
> We need to return to the topic of....
> How does this relate to our agenda item?
> We're off track. Can we get back to...?
>
> (Regulating participation)
> So, what you're telling us is...? (regulate high verbal)
> Can you summarize your point? (regulate high verbal)
> What is your opinion, Mary? (encourage low verbal)
>
> (Announcing time limits)
> Our meeting should last one hour. It will end at 2:30.
> We have 10 minutes left. Do we want to go to the next agenda item?
> Only five minutes remain. Our time is up; shall we table this until next time?

These guiding behaviors demand more assertiveness than requesting information may. Yet, it's worth the effort because it's essential for the group to stay on track.

Summarizing

During the course of discussion, many ideas are presented, a host of evidence given, and a list of solutions proposed. Periodically, these ideas, evidence, and proposals need to be rounded up and herded into a cluster for clearer viewing. A *summary* lists items without detailed development, so they can be understood and discussed in a manageable way. Here are some phrases that can assist you:

> So far, we've heard three explanations. They are....
> The brainstorming list of solutions are....
> I'm hearing two schools of thought on this. First... and second....

Summarizing is one of the most helpful behaviors you can share with your group. It can provide structure that allows the group to see what was once too big and scattered to be recognized and understood. You can use summaries to terminate or regulate run-on discussions too. It also lets participants know someone is listening and their points have been made.

Analyzing Evidence and Testing Reasoning

The sixth guiding behavior is analyzing evidence and testing reasoning. As mentioned earlier, the need for careful and thoughtful analysis of evidence and reasoning is crucial in the problem-solving process. You need to be able and willing to analyze the evidence presented and test the reasoning of the proposals set forth. Here are ways you can analyze evidence and test reasoning:

> (Analyzing evidence)
> Do you have additional evidence for this position? (testing quantity)
> What makes this researcher qualified? (testing quality)
> When was the article published? (testing recency)
> How does this relate to our topic? (testing relevancy)
>
> (Testing reasoning)
> Have we looked at enough examples to explain this event? (testing overgeneralization)
> Are there other causes that would explain this event? (testing causal fallacy)
> Are these two situations similar enough to warrant comparison? (testing false analogy)
> Could there be other positions? (testing either-or thinking)
> Let's keep this discussion on issues, not personalities. (testing ad hominem attack)

Analysis of evidence and reasoning is the hallmark of critical thinking. I cannot overstate your responsibility to test the thinking and information of your group. Without diligent effort on your part in analyzing evidence and testing the reasoning of arguments, the group's effectiveness will be compromised. Discover the detective within you.

Negotiating

We all possess the capacity to suspend personal judgment and appreciate the benefits of different points of view. Negotiating is the skill of bringing differing parties to mutual agreement, and you'll find this skill particularly valuable as the group gets closer to consensus. These negotiating skills are also helpful in settling minor conflicts and differences throughout the course of discussion. Here are some ways you can help in the negotiating process:

> Can we all agree that...? Do we all think/feel...? Is anyone opposed to...? What things can we all agree to? Can we combine the strengths of these two proposals? Is this solution workable and acceptable to all of us? Can we all live with this solution for a period of time?

Your ability and willingness to negotiate and serve as a consensus builder will be one of the most important contributions to the success of the group. Try to see the beauty and strengths in all the ideas and proposals presented to the group. Be positive and constantly alert to any common ground—areas of agreement, common ideas, and similar beliefs—where your group can meet as one.

SOCIAL GUIDING BEHAVIORS

Social guiding behaviors encourage and maintain a healthy social dimension during group discussion. They include encouraging, expressing feelings, harmonizing, and energizing. Each behavior is designed to ensure a friendly, supportive, and trusting atmosphere within the group.

Encouraging

Many times group members need encouragement to continue speaking, participating, or even remaining in the group. Encouragement fosters a caring, supportive group atmosphere. You can be encouraging to others by acknowledging their presence, agreeing with their statements, complimenting their behaviors, or reframing negatives into positives. Some things you can say to encourage others are:

(Acknowledging)
I'm glad you're here today, Ingrid! I see your point, Seth!
(Agreeing)
I agree with you, Frank. Your comment makes sense to me.
(Complimenting)
I appreciate the handouts you prepared for us, Sarah. Your idea is wonderful!
(Reframing negatives into positives)
Another way of looking at this is _____. (positive interpretation)
By pointing this out, you showed me some positive aspects, such as _____.

When you participate in a discussion, look for ways to encourage others. We all need encouragement and compliments. Discover the part of you that nurtures, cares, and supports others. It can also be an enriching experience for you, the encourager.

Expressing Feelings

The oil of interpersonal relationships is the sharing of feelings. Although your problem-solving group is not a therapy group, the expression of feelings and the acknowledgment of those feelings is essential to a healthy social dimension of any group. Whether it's to congratulate the group's successes or explore the group's interpersonal conflicts, the expression of feelings is crucial to the health and maintenance of the group. Here are some ways to encourage the expression of emotions:

How are we feeling right now?
Are you guys feeling as frustrated as I am? Maybe we need a break.
I love being in this group.

Many groups avoid expressing any emotion. They incorrectly believe such disclosure is inappropriate to the group process or a sign of weakness. Nothing could be further from the truth. Without some gauge to measure the social dimension of the members, the group will not know when to devote attention to resolving an interpersonal conflict, celebrate a task success, or merely take a much-needed five-minute break. Do what you can to encourage the expression of feelings within the group.

Harmonizing

Occasionally a disruption appears in an otherwise supportive and friendly group atmosphere. The tension or conflict between two or more members rises to a level that affects the group's task dimension effectiveness. Whether it's a disagreement over a substantive issue, hurt feelings due to an insensitive remark, or a minor feud between two individuals, the social dimension of the group is negatively affected. You should make some attempt to bring harmony back to the group. Here are some things you can say to reestablish harmony:

> Maybe the two of you can discuss this matter after the meeting.
> Let's not allow our feelings get the best of us.
> Can you two disagree without disliking one another?
> We need to focus on the issues, not personalities.

Continued conflict needs to be brought to the attention of the group. To ignore or deny its existence would give the conflict more power to disrupt the social dimension. Therefore, the initial intervention is to bring the tension or conflict to the conscious awareness of the group. Then the individuals involved can strive to discover some way to disagree without disliking, punishing, or hurting one another. We will cover specific ways to deal with this in greater detail in a later chapter. For now, however, you might want to try some harmonizing behavior when there is tension or conflict within the group.

Energizing

Working with other people in a small group can be psychologically, emotionally, and physically draining. Extended periods of time spent discussing, debating, and deliberating is taxing and can quickly deplete our energy levels and exhaust our enthusiasm. When you sense that the vitality of the group is slipping, you can try to energize the group by saying:

> We've done well so far and we only have a little ways to go!
> I think we're doing a great job!
> I know we can accomplish what we've set out to do!

There are no magic words you can chant or somersaults you can perform that guarantee bringing a group to life. But your attempt at energizing the group can be inspiring in and of itself. Enthusiasm is contagious! Choose to be the source of energy when the rest of the group is ready for a nap—you might be surprised at your impact on the group's enthusiasm.

Now that we've examined some ways to develop and enhance your group's social dimension, we can turn to a special set of guiding behaviors that address dysfunctional behavior of group members.

DYSFUNCTIONAL GUIDING BEHAVIORS

When an individual's behavior disrupts or affects the group in a negative way for an extended period of time, you might consider using some of the approaches outlined in this section. *Dysfunctional behavior* is any habitual behavior that disrupts the task and/or social functioning of the group.

Generally, you cannot deal effectively with dysfunctional behaviors using the harmonizing behaviors just mentioned. The causes of dysfunctional behavior are deeply ingrained and beyond the scope of this book. Yet you can try to bring the behavior to the attention of the individual or use some interventions that can help correct the dysfunctional behavior.

Recall that the five dysfunctional patterns of behavior or roles are the controller, blamer, pleaser, distractor, and ghost. Each role can be detrimental to the functioning of a problem-solving group.

The Controller

The *controller* tries to dominate, regulate, and manipulate group interaction. His verbal communication patterns are usually issuing orders and directives. He tends to give directions and explain the superiority of his ideas and solutions over all others presented. The controller often uses logical appeals and intricate reasoning to get his way. He can be a master of words and persuasion. He blocks and redirects discussion for his own purposes. His nonverbal posture is often rigid, tight, and stern.

Level 1 controller intervention.   The controller tries to dominate the discussion by speaking at length, interrupting others, and repeatedly bringing the discussion back to his point of view. If you notice a member displaying this type of characteristic behavior, you can:

> Summarize what the controller has said.
> State your own opinion when the controller pauses for breath.
> Ask the other group members for their input or feedback.
> Respond to his interrupting by saying, "Were you aware I was speaking?"

Level 2 controller intervention.   If the controller reacts in a hostile fashion to level 1 interventions or continues to exhibit controlling behavior, you might use level 2 interventions. The purpose of level 2 interventions is to confront the controller directly. Don't call him names or blame him directly. Your best strategy is to confront the controller personally, away from the group, and share your perceptions of his behavior. Ask him for his feedback on your perceptions to initiate a dialogue so that you can request him to (1) give more speaking time to the other group members and (2) actively listen to them. A controller will not readily give up his attempts at control, however. Be prepared to confront him again at future discussions. The important point is to label his controlling transactions while he is performing them. Here are some ways you can confront the controller:

> You've been talking about your idea for eight minutes and I'm concerned that other points of view aren't being expressed.
> When I'm (or another member) talking you seem to be interrupting. You're interrupting....
> You're bringing the discussion back to your idea. Have we discussed this enough, group?

The Blamer

The *blamer* usually finds fault with others and their ideas and suggestions, although she won't usually offer suggestions of her own. She generally blames others for the shortcomings and failures of the group. She will cast a shadow of doubt and gloom upon the solutions proposed and will be the first to say "I told you so" when a solution fails. Although she will rarely admit a mistake or failure, the blamer almost relishes casting fault on others. She'll slouch in her chair and throw her arms in the air. Everyone's to blame but her! And she told you so.

Level 1 blamer intervention.   If a group member constantly blames or complains, the first intervention is to have her provide more information to support her point. Second, ask other group members for their perceptions. Present your perceptions of the event or person being discussed. Have the group discuss one specific issue at a time. Don't let the blamer scatter the focus of the group by changing the subject with a different complaint or individual to blame. Keep the discussion focused.

Level 2 blamer intervention.   If the blamer continues to blame and complain, even relishing the additional time and attention the group has provided her with level 1 interventions, you need to change your strategy. The first thing you can do is call attention to her blaming behavior by more directly labeling her transactions: "You're blaming again" or "You're complaining again." Second, you can use a paradoxical intervention by out-blaming the blamer. Imitate the blamer during discussion by blaming others constantly. This can be tricky because the blamer might join forces with your theatrical blaming and really get on a roll. But usually, the blamer will not know how to handle the imbalance of having two blamers in the same group, and she might be forced to play a different role. Third, you can confront the blamer as a group and share your feelings about her behavior.

It is never easy to correct blaming behavior. The best you can do for the group is to bring the behavior out in the open by labeling the blaming transactions. There's something about bringing behaviors into the open that can help to modify the blamer's behavior.

The Pleaser

The *pleaser* attempts to avoid conflict and confrontation by giving in to the wishes of the others. He agrees to just about anything the others ask or require. And when a conflict begins to surface, the pleaser does whatever it takes to dissolve or neutralize the disagreement. The pleaser is generally uncomfortable asserting his own opinion, defending his position, and sharing his feelings. He backs down rather than fights. And he agrees to just about anything for the sake of peace and tranquility.

Level 1 pleaser intervention.   When an individual constantly placates and attempts to please other group members (usually the controller), you can modify his behavior by playing the "heavy." Normally, when a pleaser pleases or placates, no one intervenes and the cycle is reinforced. You can challenge the pleaser by stating positions and making demands that are the opposite of what the pleaser is agreeing to. No matter what the pleaser is agreeing to, take the opposite position (generally against the controller) and see what the rest of the group does with your intervention. Your goal is to throw the pleaser off balance by not agreeing too quickly with the pleaser's characteristic behavior. Continue this intervention when the pleaser tries to please.

Level 2 pleaser intervention.   If the pleaser continues to please, despite your contrary interventions, you can employ a different strategy. Once again, you can use a paradoxical intervention. You can "out-please the pleaser." When he agrees to a position or request of the controller, you agree with that position or request, but you advocate a more extreme position in the same direction. For instance, the controller says the group should continue the meeting, even though the rest of the group is clearly exhausted. You can agree with the pleaser, but go a step further by saying the group should continue the meeting for one more hour rather than 30 minutes. State your request in a sincere fashion and see what happens. You'll be surprised to discover how powerful paradoxical interventions can be.

The Distractor

The *distractor* doesn't give in, blame, or control. Her role is to draw or deflect the attention away from the issue at hand. When the group experiences stress or conflict, the distractor will usually joke about the situation or redirect the discussion to an unrelated issue or topic. Often the distractor is just as uncomfortable with conflict as the pleaser, but her method for handling her discomfort is different. Whereas the pleaser will placate or give in, the distractor will utilize some avoidance technique to change the subject. The distractor will attempt to sidetrack the group's work. She will joke, flirt, or question the importance of the task at hand. She is often the court jester, the class clown. For an occasional tension release, she's fine. But as a continual disturbance, her behavior can be frustrating and detrimental to the group's functioning.

Level 1 distractor intervention.   The best way to deal with a constant distractor is to ignore her diverting comments and request that the group return to the discussion topic. Remember to label her transactions by saying, "You're distracting us from the topic at hand. Can we return to our discussion?" Be swift in making your request to return to the discussion after the distractor makes her statement, even though she might object to your being "too serious" or "too uptight." Ignore humorous or sarcastic remarks from the distractor; simply make your request to "return to the discussion."

Level 2 distractor intervention.   If the distractor refuses to cooperate by continuing her distracting behavior, you should bring the matter to the group for discussion. Share your perceptions of her distracting behavior and how you feel about its dysfunctional effect upon the group. Ask for feedback from the other members of the group. Most likely, the distractor will use humor or divert the attention of the group by shifting blame to something or someone else (namely you for being too serious). Your interventions should be able to modify or eliminate her distracting behavior.

The Ghost

The final dysfunctional role is the *ghost*. Just as the word suggests, this group member cannot be seen. Whether he's sitting with the group or has missed the meeting again, he contributes nothing to the group. Like a silent face in the crowd, the ghost sits there in the group and say nothing. The cause of this behavior may be stage fright, lack of commitment, apathy, or a host of other explanations. But the result is always the same. He's the group member who doesn't participate or show up. The ghost has been called the nonperformer, the low-verbal, and the passive-aggressive personality. I simply refer to him as the ghost, because he's not really there. Yet his impact on the group's task effectiveness and social atmosphere can be devastating.

Level 1 ghost intervention.   Of all five dysfunctional behaviors, this one is the most difficult to prescribe an intervention for because of the variety of reasons that might be causing his behavior. Without going into a more involved and detailed discussion of these reasons, I'd like to suggest some simple guidelines for dealing with this behavior:

> Encourage the ghost (silent or low-verbal member) to share his opinion.
> Compliment the ghost for any contributions.
> Take the ghost out for coffee after a meeting. Be friendly.
> Confront the ghost for not following through on duties.
> Confront the ghost for not attending a meeting.

Level 2 ghost intervention.   If the ghost continues to remain a silent (or low-verbal) group member, maybe that's his personal or cultural style of communication. There are individuals who are, by nature or past experience, more reticent than others, and you have to find gentle ways to encourage their participation. There are also individuals whose cultural or ethnic background differ from ours in terms of interaction expectations. Many cultures regard direct eye contact, personal remarks and requests, and individual achievement as undesirable and objectionable. You should be sensitive to these differences in cultural perspective and still discover ways to invite and promote participation in the group.

Of the five dysfunctional roles, the ghost can be the most difficult individual to accurately and effectively deal with. Be tentative, gentle, supportive, and sensitive with him, but enforce rules that govern completion of tasks and attendance. Neglecting responsibilities and absences from meetings cannot be tolerated indefinitely. If in doubt, be kind but firm.

These five dysfunctional roles may arise occasionally in your group. The behavior of those exhibiting any of these roles will normally be mild and subtle, requiring only one or two interventions on your part to modify or eliminate them. But if the behavior is extreme, exaggerated, or physically threatening, appropriate steps should be taken to release the individual from the group.

This chapter suggested specific ways you can guide a discussion by performing certain behaviors. They were tasking guiding behaviors, social guiding behaviors, and dysfunctional guiding behaviors. These guiding behaviors are effective ways to promote more effective discussions within your group. You do not have to be the leader of the group to lead and influence the other group members. Your use of these guiding behaviors will empower you to keep the discussion focused, productive, and ultimately, successful.

INDIVIDUAL AND GROUP EXERCISES

Exercise 7.1   Guiding Behavior in Your Personal Life

Use one or two of the task guiding behaviors from this chapter and implement them in your relationships with others. For instance, you might want to ask people more questions (requesting or clarifying information), compromise your positions (negotiating), or think more critically (analyzing). See how that feels in your daily interactions with those individuals in your life.

Exercise 7.2   Group Role-Playing

Have a group member role-play one of the five dysfunctional behavior roles in a problem-solving activity. After the role-player has played his part in the problem-solving activity, the other group members attempt to modify his behavior using the interventions suggested. Have each group member role-play a dysfunctional role. How did your group handle the various roles? Can you see yourself actually using these interventions in a real-life situation? Why or why not?

E I G H T
LEADING A GROUP

Leading well means serving well.
–Van Cummings

Fran didn't look like a leader to me. She was petite, about five feet tall, and weighed maybe 95 pounds. Her voice was soft, and when she took her seat at the conference table during the group's initial meeting, she appeared to be a head lower than the rest of us.

Fran was a new faculty member, clearly one of the youngest in our group. She looked almost like a student sitting at that oversized, wooden table in the president's conference room. The seven of us had been appointed by the president of our college to propose ways to market our institution to the local community.

There was no proposed agenda and no designated leader. Only the seven of us scheduled to meet eight times during the semester. Six of us knew each other from years past, but we didn't know Fran. However, during the following decade, Fran was going to become very well known to us—she would become our college president.

What makes an effective leader? Well, it depends. Each task and every group are different. And what works in one setting may not work in another. But there are some common denominators that are characteristic of an effective small group leader. And I observed them in Fran's interactions with us in that committee many years ago.

Fran's foremost purpose in every meeting was to serve the committee, not further her own agenda, ideas, or proposals. She brought out the best in each of us by consistently demonstrating those guiding skills and behaviors discussed in Chapter 7. Fran would gently guide us back on track when we wandered, summarize the various points when we got long-winded, and negotiate consensus when we hovered near agreement. She prepared handouts and visual aids for the group and even brought donuts to a meeting or two.

All these things she did without fanfare—without requiring the limelight or special thanks; without our becoming jealous of her skills; without really anything. Although other members brainstormed better ideas or debated with greater skill, it was Fran who consistently and unselfishly brought out the best in each of us. She sincerely and deeply wanted the best for the group. The effective leader is the one who serves the group well—to help the group realize its goal.

Leadership is the focus of this chapter. We will examine approaches to leadership, functions of leadership, how to lead an effective meeting, and how to take care of yourself as a leader. The underlying theme of this chapter is that you can participate in the leadership of any problem-solving group. The leadership skills you develop in this chapter will help you discover the leader within.

WHAT IS LEADERSHIP?

Since the beginning of time, people in groups have listened to the counsel, followed the suggestions, and even looked up to specific individuals within the tribe, hamlet, community, or organization. These individuals are the leaders of the group. Whether inherited, won by battle or election, or arrived at by group consensus, leadership has been a focus of attention and interest throughout history. For the purposes of this book, however, we will limit our discussion to the leadership of small groups assigned to solve a problem.

First, what is a leader? A *leader* is an individual who is perceived by group members as having a legitimate position of power or influence in the group. The leader can be assigned or designated to that position. Or the leader may emerge from within the group's interactive process or even by group election.

Leadership, however, is different. *Leadership* is the process of influencing the task and social dimensions of a group to help it reach its goal. By this definition, leadership can involve more than one individual. All group members can share leadership.

Each individual in the group has the potential and opportunity to participate in the leadership functions of the group. Although this chapter provides specific and practical suggestions for a designated leader to more effectively run a meeting or manage a small group, it emphasizes ways each group member can help the group reach its goal.

APPROACHES TO LEADERSHIP

Before we discuss the characteristics and process skills required of an effective small group leader, we need to briefly review the four most prevalent approaches to studying leadership. They are the trait, styles, situational, and functional approaches to leadership.

Trait Approach

The trait approach suggests that individuals are born with certain personality traits that make them good leaders. In the past, physical traits such as attractiveness, height, a deep voice, and a full head of hair were linked or perceived as predictors or requirements for leadership. Personality traits such as achievement orientation, self-confidence, intelligence, enthusiasm, adaptability, sociability, and responsibility were also perceived as required traits for leaders. The trait approach implicitly suggests that most of these traits are characteristics an individual is born with. Thus, the "born leader" illustrates the trait approach to understanding why certain individuals become leaders.

This approach to understanding leadership has not been a successful determinant of leadership emergence. There are scores of famous leaders, and leaders you have experienced in your personal life, who do not possess many of the physical and psychological requirements set forth by the trait approach. Group process is too intricate and diverse, and personality too complex, to be so easily explained.

Styles Approach

The second approach to understanding leadership is the styles approach, which examines how an individual leads rather than why a certain individual becomes the leader. The three styles of leadership are autocratic, democratic, and laissez-faire.

Autocratic leadership. The autocratic leader rules with firm control over the group process. She generally sees herself as the leader and the rest of the group as followers. Often, the autocratic leader will listen to the ideas and suggestions of the other group members or subordinates, but the ultimate decision-making process rests more with her than with the group. She believes she knows what's best for the group and expects the others to follow and support what she feels is the wisest course of action. The autocratic leader will often use a variety of methods to enforce her decisions and establish compliance within the group.

Democratic leader.   This style of leadership emphasizes the participation of group members in discussion and decision-making. The democratic leader recognizes the value of group input and participation, and seeks the majority opinion, or consensus. Emphasis is placed on the group and the democratic leader leads by example, not by force.

Laissez-faire leader.   The laissez-faire leader lets the group lead itself. Whether the leader selects this style because she is uncomfortable leading others or believes that her leadership will have counterproductive effects on the group, she chooses to operate from a "hands-off" approach. She will generally see herself as just another group member and will not attempt to enforce or exercise her position as leader. Instead, she will let the members engage in the work themselves.

These three styles of leadership have advantages and disadvantages. Research has shown the most productive styles can be the autocratic and democratic approaches to leadership. The autocratic style produces more efficiently run groups, which complete tasks in less time. The democratic style produces the greatest member satisfaction, but requires more time to complete tasks. The laissez-faire style is effective with groups of extremely independent or creative members who require a great deal of freedom and latitude in performance.

Current research on group productivity and member satisfaction confirms the notion that the democratic style of leadership appears to be the most effective approach to leading a group (Schultz, 1996). I've found from my personal experience that a democratic style of leadership usually produces higher member satisfaction and productivity than do the autocratic and laissez-faire styles. Keep in mind that the leader's communication skills and relationship with group members are important determinants of group success, regardless of leadership style.

Situational Approach

The third approach to leadership study is the situational approach, which stresses that the requirements for effective leadership depend upon the situation. In the situational approach groups locate the relevant characteristics of the situation and determine what kind of leadership style and personality would be the most effective in achieving the specific goals.

The requirements of the task to be performed determine which style would be most appropriate. Leading a therapy group would require a different style of leadership than, say, a commando unit behind enemy lines or a preschool parents meeting. The attributes or characteristics of the group can also determine what would work best to lead the group. A club of retired millionaires, a group of medical students, and a collection of prisoners might all demand different styles and personality characteristics of its leader for optimum performance and satisfaction. And finally, an individual's knowledge and experience play a role in determining who emerges or is called on to lead, depending upon the tasks and constraints of a particular situation.

Functional Approach

The functional approach offers a different way of looking at leadership. It examines the communication behaviors of any group member that leads the group closer to its goal. Beatrice Schultz defines functional leadership as "a process in which a leader engages in many behaviors, both verbal and nonverbal, to help a group achieve a goal." Rather than pay attention to the characteristics of the leader, the style of leadership, or the situation within which the leader must emerge, the functional approach focuses on the individual acts that influence the task and social dimensions of the group and move the group toward its goal.

FUNCTIONS OF LEADERSHIP

The functional approach provides us with a useful framework to understand and develop our leadership skills. There are more complex models of leadership available, but for our purposes, the functional approach will enable you to communicate and work as an effective leader in any small group.

Chapter 7 suggested 11 specific communication behaviors that influence the task and social dimensions of the group to reach its goal.

1. Requesting information	7. Negotiating
2. Providing information	8. Encouraging
3. Clarifying information	9. Expressing feelings
4. Guiding discussion	10. Harmonizing
5. Summarizing	11. Energizing
6. Analyzing	

In addition to these guiding behaviors, five other guiding behaviors and interventions were provided to address an individual's chronic dysfunctional behavior in group discussion. Combined, these 16 behaviors give an individual a wide variety of communication behaviors, to help the group reach its goal.

LEADING AN EFFECTIVE MEETING

One of the most important functional skills of any leader is to lead an effective meeting. Many specific skills and behaviors go into running a meeting that is productive, organized, and even enjoyable. Here are 20 suggestions for you to lead an effective meeting.

1. Clarify the leader's job description. Before you volunteer, are appointed, or elected as the leader of a group, you need to clarify the duties and responsibilities of the position. Consult your boss, supervisor, group, or an appropriate source to review what is expected of you in this leadership role. Get the job description in writing if possible. What are the expected time lines for projects? When does this position end? Under what circumstances can you be replaced? What special things should you know about the duties, the group members, or the project you will be in charge of?

2. Consider if you want to be the leader. Take the next two days and weigh the pros and cons of being the leader of this specific group. After considering the duties, responsibilities, and time expected of you, you need to be honest with yourself. Is this something you really want to do? Is this something you really need to do? Or is this just another feather in your cap? A way to receive recognition or exercise power? Honestly consider your motives. You should ask yourself if this is a position in which you would want to serve others—the group members and the organization.

If you've never led a group before, don't be afraid to accept the position or nomination. Every great leader had a first leadership position. This could be yours! If you decide to accept the position, you will discover many wonderful things about yourself and others. You might also experience moments of disappointment, stress, failure, and disillusionment. All this comes with the territory.

3. Determine to meet or not to meet. Once you are in a position of leadership in a problem-solving group, you will need to have your group meet. Most of the time, the meeting times and dates are determined for you. But if they're not, you will need to contact your group members and negotiate meeting times and dates.

After the scheduled meetings have begun, you might occasionally determine that certain future meetings do not require members' physical presence, and the information or business can be communicated or conducted by phone, memo, or fax. Take every opportunity to conduct the group's business in the most expedient fashion possible. Use the phone, mail, and fax to your advantage. If you decide not to convene a meeting, your group members will love you for it.

4. Prepare and send the agenda before the meeting. If possible, prepare and send a copy of the meeting's agenda (and any pertinent reading material) to each group member one week *before* the meeting. This gives ample time for group members to read, consider, and even research appropriate material before you meet. I usually have a rule when I chair a group that members cannot verbally participate in discussions if they haven't read the agenda *and* other material *before* the meeting. This prevents members from shuffling paper and reading material during discussion.

The following is an example of a generic meeting agenda. You might want to refer to it when constructing your own agenda:

AGENDA
1. Call to order.
2. Approve agenda.
3. Approve minutes from previous meeting.
4. Announcements.
5. Reports (officers and committees).
6. Old (unfinished) business. List all items that will be before the group for discussion or action.
7. New business.
8. Adjournment.

5. Limit and prioritize the agenda items.   When you construct the agenda, limit the number of items you schedule the group to address and discuss. I know a group leader who limits each meeting to just one item or issue. Not two or three. One. He swears by this method. It's a little extreme, but I would rather err in his direction than have too many agenda items. A group needs focus, so limit the number of discussion items in new and old business.

Prioritize your agenda items starting from the most important, in terms of significance and weight, to the least important. That way, if your group doesn't get to the last item or two, you have at least addressed the higher-priority items. You'll have other meetings.

6. Envision what will happen at the meeting.   Take a few moments and try to envision what will happen at the meeting. Close your eyes and visualize each group member at the meeting. See as many details of this mental picture as possible. Keep your eyes closed. Relax. And get a sense of what you want to happen.

7. Arrive early.   Arrive 10 to 15 minutes early to the meeting. Arrange the chairs in a circle, check the lighting, open windows if it's stuffy, and plug in the coffee maker. No, a secretary or assistant isn't supposed to do this—remember, effective leadership means effective service. Get a feel for the atmosphere of the room before people begin arriving.

8. Mingle with the members.   As the group members arrive, mingle, join in, and make them feel welcome. Thank people individually for coming early. Listen to them and be really present in mind and body.

9. Start the meeting on time.   About two minutes before the scheduled meeting time, announce to group members the meeting is about to begin. Invite them to get another cup of coffee and move to your seat. After they see you seated, they will usually follow. *Begin the meeting exactly on time!* This is the first official act you perform each meeting. Don't be sloppy or indecisive with this initial responsibility.

10. Make announcements quickly.   After everyone is seated, get any announcements that weren't included in the agenda out of the way as quickly as possible. Announcements are not open to debate or discussion. Briefly answer any questions about the announcements. This is not the time to get bogged down with tangential remarks and off-the-track discussions.

11. State the meeting objectives and time limits.   Thank the group members for attending the meeting and for being punctual. Then state the objective or objectives for the meeting. Provide a tentative time limit for each objective or agenda item, and state the ending time for the meeting. Group members appreciate a leader who will publicly announce the time limits for agenda items and the ending time of the meeting. It gets things out in the open and provides a framework for discussion.

12. Don't stop the meeting for latecomers.   Occasionally, a group member will arrive late to the meeting. Don't recap what's already been covered and don't acknowledge or listen to her excuse for being late. Simply ensure that the discussion continues without giving attention to the latecomer. Chronic tardiness can be a symptom of passive-aggressive behavior (indirect anger directed at you or the group) or a challenge to your power. Don't give the chronic latecomer any power.

13. Restate objectives and time limits periodically.   About every 10 minutes, restate the objective the group is currently working on and how many minutes are left in the meeting. If possible, avoid holding any meeting for more than 60 minutes. Human beings get tired and bored after one hour.

14. Remain impartial.   As the leader, your primary goal is to ensure the smooth functioning of the task and social dimensions of the group. Let all group members voice their opinions on a particular issue before you share your thoughts. Your duty is to solicit and guide the group's discussion so it stays on track and on time. Your job is to serve the group.

15. Guiding the group.   The specific guiding behaviors you can draw upon to guide group discussion are discussed in detail in Chapter 7 and reviewed at the beginning of this chapter. Keep a note card summary of these guiding behaviors in front of you during each meeting as a reminder.

16. Seek participation.   Even though asking for information is one of the guiding behaviors mentioned in item 14, I want to stress its importance. Ask for the opinions of low-verbal members and summarize the long speeches of high-verbal members. Your group needs to know and experience your control of the group. They need to see you provide equal (at least not lopsided) group participation. Be sensitive to who's not talking and who's talking too much.

17. Summarize often.   I know I mentioned the guiding behaviors already, but I need to bring this one up again. Occasional summaries can work wonders to focus discussion, to quiet high-verbals, and to keep the group on time. Look for opportune moments to summarize the group's ideas and progress.

18. Compliment members often.   See the positive in the contributions and participation of each member. Verbally compliment individuals during the meeting. Someone once said, "A person can accomplish a great deal if he doesn't worry about who gets the credit." Don't worry about who ultimately gets credit for anything the group does. Give the credit (and compliments) liberally to your group members. You will not only boost their feelings of importance, you will encourage participation and encourage member loyalty to you.

19. Keep the meeting moving.   Don't get bogged down on any one item or issue too long. Table items to the next meeting if additional information is required or if the tension in the group is getting too great. Remember to summarize and state the time remaining in the meeting. During the last five minutes of the meeting, I usually give time-remaining announcements a couple of times: "We've got four minutes left," "We've got two minutes left," and so on.

20. End the meeting on time.   If you conclude the meeting on time, you will be establishing one of the most powerful norms of group work. That norm is "This leader ends when she says she will end, so I'd better get what I want to say in and accomplish what I intend to accomplish during the time or I'll have to wait until the next meeting." Or stated another way, the norm you establish is *"This leader keeps her promises."*

End the meeting on time and your group members will love you for it. Each member has a life outside the group (at least you hope they do). So end on time and let them get on with their lives. During the last minute or so of each meeting, I summarize the objective or objectives we've accomplished and remind them of the next meeting time and date.

TAKING CARE OF YOURSELF AS THE LEADER

The duties and responsibilities of a leadership position can be psychologically taxing, emotionally fatiguing, and physically draining. Whether you're the president of a large corporation or the head of the Little League pancake breakfast, the job of leading a group of people can push you to the limits of your capabilities and patience.

To avoid leader burnout, I'd like to suggest some ways to take good care of yourself when you're the leader of a problem-solving group. These are attitudes you can adopt and things you can do to remain centered, open, and productive in your role as leader.

1. Leave some things to others. My first suggestion is to volunteer or accept a position of leadership only for a group whose purpose you believe in deep in your heart. Life will go on without you as the leader, so don't feel obligated to volunteer for a leadership position you don't believe in.

If you really don't believe in and support the functions and purpose of the local Little League Organization, don't volunteer to chair the pancake breakfast committee. You can serve as a member of the committee out of a sense of obligation if your child or little brother is on a team, but don't volunteer to chair the committee if your heart's not in it.

I realize there are some situations where you might not have a choice, such as in your job, where a boss or supervisor assigns the responsibilities of leadership to you. In those instances, you can still choose to discuss your concerns or misgivings with your boss. Maybe you will be successful in changing your boss's mind. If not, you can choose to utilize the skills and understanding you've gained from this book and lead with a positive attitude.

Life is short. Try to put your energy into those things you believe to be important and lasting. A friend of mine believes each of us is born with only a certain number of breaths for our lifetime. Once that magic number is reached, we die. Not a breath before. Not a breath after. And for each person, this number is different. How many breaths do you have left? How do you want to spend your remaining breaths? Lead only those groups you believe in.

2. Leave your ego at the door. As the leader of a group, you will often be the target of criticism when things go wrong, the butt of jokes behind your back, and the last one to know if members are dissatisfied with your performance. In extreme instances, individuals and coalitions within your group can assail your recommendations, find fault with your style of leading, and attack your character. The price of leadership can be high.

You will need to discover ways to detach from your ego if you are to be an effective leader. Once you enter the meeting room, you will have to leave your ego at the door, or forever be pulled and tugged, hurt and angered by every questioning remark and critical suggestion directed toward you during the heat of discussion. Remember, you're not paid to be their friend. Your role is to lead.

3. Leave time for other things.   Obsession is one of the most common mistakes leaders make. They do nothing but eat, think, and sleep their role as leader. The leadership position consumes their days and haunts their nights. To avoid this, make sure you leave time in your daily life for other things. Talk with loved ones and friends about anything other than your problem-solving task. Take up a new sport or hobby. Spend more time with your spouse or children doing things you meant to do last summer. See more matinee movies during the week. Take walks around the neighborhood and make some new acquaintances. Teach your dog new tricks. Do things to balance your life.

4. Leave the paddle at home.   Self-doubt, self-criticism, and self-punishment can cripple and immobilize even the best of leaders. No one is perfect. We all make mistakes. No leader is blameless or beyond error. We need to accept our faults and weaknesses, as well as our strengths. When you become a leader of a group, don't be too demanding on yourself. Don't beat yourself up after every minor mistake. Be gentler on yourself. Leave the paddle at home.

5. Leave room to learn.   One marvelous way to look at all problems and conflicts with others is to see them as an opportunity to learn a lesson about yourself.

Suppose some jerk tries to push into your lane during a traffic jam. Cars are at a standstill and she aims her front bumper toward your car and creeps in your direction. She doesn't smile at you or even make any eye contact to acknowledge her intentions. She thinks she owns the road. Well, you could pull up to prevent her entry into that tiny space between you and the car in front of you. You could honk and communicate your annoyance. You could yell something really terrible to her. You could even aim your car in her direction and play a little two-mile-per-hour chicken. You could do all kinds of terrible things in this difficult situation.

But another way you can look at it is as a lesson to learn something wonderful about yourself. I know this may sound a little corny, but it can work wonders. You can see this situation as an opportunity to learn unselfish, altruistic courtesy and kindness. You can let the jerk (I mean, person) into the space in front of you.

This used to sound unthinkable to me a few years ago, but since I've been trying to take this new approach to driving and actually let people pull in front of me, I've changed a little. I have learned I'm capable of being kind in a situation when I could be rude and vindictive. I've learned to be courteous and not even expect a brief wave of thanks from the driver. I've learned to let people have the space I once occupied. I've learned to let go a little more. And it's made all the difference in the world.

I've taken an old problem and chosen to see it as a way to learn to be a little kinder to others, without expecting anything in return. This is how you can also choose to view the problems and conflicts you may experience as the leader of a group. During your tenure as leader, people will aim their cars at you, wanting things you might not want to give up. But choose not to see it always as a challenge to fight, or an opportunity to assert your power. See it as an invitation to learn some new things about yourself.

As the group leader, be open to discovering the many untapped skills, characteristics, and talents that still lay hidden from your conscious mind. You are much more complicated, competent, and caring than you think. Be open to discovering more and more about yourself as you lead others.

In this chapter we focused on the subject of group leadership. We examined approaches to leadership, functions of leadership, how to lead an effective meeting, and how to take care of yourself as a leader. One important assumption we made is that any member of the group can participate in the leadership functions—those behaviors that help the group reach its goal. I hope the leadership skills you gained from this chapter will help you discover the leader within.

INDIVIDUAL AND GROUP EXERCISES

Exercise 8.1   Interview a Leader

Select a leader you have worked with in the past or present who you feel is an effective leader. This individual could be a project manager, a committee chairperson, a supervisor at work, a coach, a personnel director, a scoutmaster, the president of your PTA, and so on. Arrange for a 15-minute interview to gather his or her insights concerning leadership. Review the suggestions for interviewing presented in Chapter 6 before you request the interview. Here are some possible questions for your interview:

> What is the single most important lesson you learned from leading others?
> What do you like best about leadership?
> What do you like least about leadership?
> What do you do to increase the group's task effectiveness?
> What do you do to increase the group's social effectiveness?
> What specific suggestions could you give for becoming an effective leader?

How did your interview go? Did you remember to send a thank-you card? What things did you learn about leadership from your interview? Are there any suggestions or insights you could incorporate into your leadership skills or knowledge? Did your perceptions or feelings about this individual change after the interview? How? What is the most important lesson you learned from interviewing this individual?

Exercise 8.2   Leadership Role-Play

Have your group work on a simple problem-solving task and select one group member to role-play an autocratic leader for 10 minutes. Then have the same individual role-play a laissez-faire leader during the next 10 minutes. And for the final 10 minutes, have the individual role-play a democratic leader. How did the group members feel about each leadership style? How did the role-player feel about playing leadership style? What did the group learn about leadership during this exercise?

N I N E
BUILDING A COHESIVE GROUP

Greet each day with love in your heart.
–Paul Sanders

L ike a million pieces of shattered glass, the soft light of the moon
sparkled on a quiet sea. The flames of the seven candles flick-
ered and danced with the warm evening breeze and our faces re-
flected the golden glow of their light. As we sat circled in our beach
chairs at the end of Gaviota Pier, I realized this was a special evening—
an evening I would remember for years to come.

This was our final meeting as a group. For the past three quarters,
the seven of us—five students and two professors—had worked together on a student/faculty advisory committee for the university's
Speech Communication Department. I was one of the five students.
Our task was to monitor student feedback on four new speech courses
and provide recommendations for their improvement.

On that particular evening, the music of our talk and laughter
surrounded us as we shared highlights of our yearlong experience.
Someone spoke of our unusual meeting places—living rooms, res-
taurants, and parks. Another expressed an appreciation for the
compliment sessions at the end of each meeting. Still another reminded us of the food and drink that accompanied each meeting. I
told the group I liked the way we got along well right from the start.

It was interesting to note that not one of the highlights mentioned
involved a decision we had made or a problem we had solved.
Rather, we spoke of things that made us feel successful, connected,
and liked. We spoke of things that gave us a feeling of being committed to one another—the social dimension of our group.

After all is said and done, the task dimension of a group is long forgotten. I don't remember one agenda item we debated. I can't recall a single decision we made. All I am left with are the good feelings the group experience gave me and how those experiences became part of who I am. These good feelings are the direct result of the cohesion experienced by the group members.

This chapter examines five ways you can build a cohesive problem-solving group and a healthy social dimension. If group members discover some level of success, connection, value, support, and trust, they will more likely experience a social dimension that produces a cohesive group.

THE SOCIAL DIMENSION

The social dimension of a group lives on long after the task has been completed. An individual's feelings of successful cooperation, connection, appreciation, support, and trust derived from the group experience can play a significant role in shaping and strengthening his or her self-concept. If the social dimension, however, is characterized by competition, apprehension, and mistrust, the group experience can impact the individual's self-concept and attitude in a negative way for years to come.

The significance of the social dimension cannot be overstated. Without a healthy, supportive social climate in which to conduct the work of the group, task effectiveness can be compromised (Fisher and Ellis, 1990; Shaw, 1981).

Whereas the goal of the group's task dimension is productivity, the goal of the social dimension is *cohesion*—the attraction and connection of group members to one another and to the group.

FEELING SUCCESSFUL

The primary reason for the problem-solving group's existence is to solve a problem. To experience success in problem-solving can contribute to building a cohesive group. Members of an athletic team who win all their games during a season will more likely feel connected to one another than will members of a team who lose every game. Successful goal attainment plays a significant role in how members feel about one another and themselves. Without experiencing some level of goal achievement, a problem-solving group often deteriorates into a collection of frustrated, disconnected, and disappointed individuals.

Here are four steps you can take to bring success to your group— agreement on the group's goal, formulation of mini-goals, emphasis on group cooperation, and achievement of personal goals.

Agreeing on the Group's Goal

The first step you can take toward success is to make certain that each group member agrees on the group's goal. A group cannot be successful in achieving a goal if confusion or disagreement exist about what that goal is.

In a technical way, this step is accomplished during the second step of the problem-solving agenda—analysis of the problem. During this phase, the group formulates the question of policy ("What should be done about...?" or "What should our policy be towards...?"). This step provides the group with its task goal. Without a clearly defined and agreed-upon goal, the group can drift aimlessly.

Formulating Mini-Goals

A simple technique you can use to make your group experience successful more often is to formulate mini-goals—breaking down the larger goal into its smaller or component parts. For instance, instead of focusing solely on eliminating neighborhood theft, the group may want to break down this larger goal into its incremental parts. Smaller goals can include gathering information from law enforcement agencies, conducting an attitude survey of neighbors, holding an informational meeting for the neighborhood, and distributing a list of possible solutions to neighbors for their input.

When I chair a problem-solving group, I construct a list of mini-goals with suggested completion dates and the name of the individual responsible for each goal. I distribute this list to group members at the beginning of each meeting, and group members announce the progress of their particular mini-goal for that session. I've found that people enjoy bragging about their mini-goal achievement and appreciate the compliments from group members.

Another advantage to formulating mini-goals is it divides the labor among the group. No individual is stuck doing all the work. When one group member, through choice or circumstance, is left with an inordinate amount of responsibility, the social dimension can suffer. It's more effective from a task point of view to utilize this division of labor and assign mini-goals to each member. Most important, it provides each individual with added opportunities to experience success during the process of attempting to achieve the larger group goal.

Emphasizing Group Cooperation

A third step you can take toward group success is to emphasize group cooperation rather than competition. A group that encourages competition among its members will often experience a social dimension characterized by mistrust, selfishness, and rivalry. When members attempt to outdo one another, or to win at the expense of someone else's loss, they threaten the group's cohesiveness. Competition creates a win-lose atmosphere. And where there are losers, there are individuals who don't feel good about themselves.

Here are two ways to emphasize cooperation within your group. First, divide the group into subgroups of two or three individuals and make each subgroup responsible for a mini-goal. This will provide members with the opportunity to work together in a smaller group setting, helping to build teamwork and intimacy. And second, you can hold what I refer to as an "expert session," where group members share a problem they might be experiencing with their mini-goal and the other group members try to provide helpful or "expert" information or advice. This also emphasizes cooperation between members.

Achieving Personal Goals

Although the primary function of each group member is to participate and contribute toward the achievement of the group goal, there are also concurrent personal needs each individual hopes to satisfy while participating in the group. Many times these personal needs are minor and incidental, such as the need to investigate a new topic, use a new communication skill, or brag about an interview. Other times, they can serve as the primary motivation or reason for seeking group membership. Loneliness, underappreciation, and a desire for control are some examples of why an individual seeks group membership to satisfy personal needs.

You can make it possible to satisfy these needs by having group members state any personal needs they may be conscious of during the orientation phase. After group members introduce themselves, I also have them state one or two personal goals they'd like to achieve during the course of our group work.

Most of the time, individuals share personal goals that can be easily achieved during the course of the group's life. I will occasionally begin a meeting with a check-in. At that time group members are given an opportunity to share any progress they made toward one or more personal goals. During the course of an hour meeting, I devote three to five minutes to this activity every third meeting. This can do wonders for building a cohesive group.

FEELING CONNECTED

A second way to build a cohesive group is to make each member feel connected to the other members. Some groups are characterized by an atmosphere of distance, coolness, and indifference, whereas other groups enjoy an atmosphere of connection, inclusion, and trust. Here are some ways you can make your group members feel connected and included in the group setting—acknowledging others, structuring an all-channel network, being interested in others, and socializing as a group.

Acknowledging Others

Before the meeting begins, welcome group members as they arrive. Greet them with a smile and use their first names. It's amazing what a smile, a handshake, and a first name will do to make someone feel welcomed and included. If a group member is not included in some of the premeeting chitchat, go over and say hello. Offer that person a cup of coffee. Ask how his or her day went. These simple acts of acknowledging someone's presence can determine the emotional experience for an individual's entire meeting. If in doubt, smile and do your best to make someone feel included and connected to the group. That can be your most important act of the entire meeting.

Structuring an All-Channel Network

Another way to make group members feel connected to the group is to structure an all-channel network system for the group process. A communication network is the arrangement of communication flow within a system. With an *all-channel network* group members have access to all the other members without having to go through a central gatekeeper. Each member is free to speak and listen directly to every other group member.

There are a number of specific steps you can take to ensure an all-channel network in your group. First, from a purely physical point of view, have the group always sit in a circle. Move the chairs or desks into a circle before the meeting begins. Request that latecomers join the circle upon arrival. A circle configuration permits contact among all members. It discourages members from feeling left out, as might be the case if the group sat in rows or at a long table.

Second, have group members exchange home and work phone numbers. This enables everyone to have access to each group member. Everyone can speak directly to everyone else.

A third thing you can do to encourage an all-channel network is to discourage dialogues between two individuals during a group discussion. Whenever two members begin to conduct an extended dialogue, interrupt them and bring the discussion back to the group. Often, two powerful group members will dominate discussion, and the group process will begin to resemble dialogue between two people rather than group communication. Don't permit this to occur. For a group to be cohesive, provide open and equal access to communication.

Being Interested in Others

Our lives are busy and we often find ourselves left with little time to become acquainted with even those we work with. Feeling connected to others can also be achieved by taking a moment or two to show an interest in another group member.

Rather than seeing others as merely cogs in the machinery, you can devote a brief period of time before and after each meeting to initiate a more personal discussion with another group member. Nothing too deep and heavy. But you can show an interest in another person by simply asking questions about family, hobbies, sports, interests, and so on. Don't force anything. Be gentle and friendly. Remember, the point is to connect with another person. The actual content of your after-meeting conversation is not nearly as important as your showing interest in another person by asking questions and listening attentively.

Socializing as a Group

Some of the most famous electronic companies in the world owe a large part of their accomplishments to their legendary Friday gatherings. Companies like Apple Computer, Tandem, National Semiconductor, and Rolm are famous for their socializing on Friday after-noons. Over food, drink, and music, employees from every level of the corporation get together informally to talk shop, socialize, and get better acquainted. They've discovered this is a wonderfully en-joyable way to have fun, become better acquainted, and solve work-related problems.

You might want to do something along these lines with your own problem-solving group. It's not necessary to throw a $5,000 bash on a Friday afternoon for the six members of your group, but you might offer to treat the group to pizza and soft drinks after the next meet-ing or bring refreshments to the meeting. You can offer your home for a potluck dinner/meeting the next time your group is scheduled to meet.

Whatever you try, look for ways to occasionally socialize with your group, after or even during the meeting. When we socialize, we change our demeanor and the group has a new frame of reference from which to work. Socializing with the group members is one of the most enjoyable and powerful ways to enhance the social dimen-sion of any collection of people.

FEELING VALUED

In addition to experiencing task success and feeling connected to the group, members need to feel valued for their effort and contribu-tions. Expressions of appreciation and compliments contribute to a strong social dimension in any group, and serve an especially vital function in building a cohesive group. When group members feel valued for their effort, their loyalty and commitment to the group are strengthened. Here are three ways you can make people feel valued in your group—seeing the best in others, communicating apprecia-tion, and sharing compliments.

Seeing the Best in Others

When was the last time you told someone you appreciated them? Have you communicated appreciation to someone in the last day? How about the past week? We are often so busy, so preoccupied, and so involved with our own lives, we neglect to notice and appre-ciate others. In your problem-solving group, you need to become more appreciative by seeing the best in others and communicating your appreciation to them.

I have a theory about life: On any given day 80 percent of our life is working well and only 20 percent of our life is not working at an acceptable level. I call it my 80/20 rule.

Roughly 80 percent of your work life, your personal relationships, your body, your automobile, your yard tools, and so on are working or performing at an acceptable level. The other 20 percent is not. And yet when you stop and think about it, we often give that 20 percent of our lives 100 percent of our attention. We become fixated on a critical remark from our boss. We obsess about someone else getting a raise. We worry about an overdrawn check. We spend a great deal of time and effort fretting about 20 percent of those things that aren't going well, while we ignore the 80 percent of our lives that is functioning well.

The 80/20 rule also operates in our problem-solving groups. We often tend to focus our attention on the 20 percent of frustrations, disappointments, and failures experienced by the group, and neglect the 80 percent that is successful.

In order to appreciate others, we need to wear new glasses. We need to look for those things, both big and little, that are working. We need to notice that everyone arrived to the meeting on time. We need to see that everyone contributed something to the discussion. We need to recognize that we made some progress on reaching consensus. We need to be aware of the subtle attempts of some members to improve how they interact during discussion. We need to see the best, not the worst, of what is happening in this moment.

Communicating Appreciation

Once you've decided to see the best in every situation—to concentrate on the 80 percent of the group process that is working well—you need to verbally communicate your appreciation. Simply make an I-statement of appreciation: "Yung, I appreciated your efforts in having us reach consensus this morning," "Alison, I appreciated the questions you asked that helped me clarify my thoughts during the meeting," and "Victor, I thank you for letting me put my report on the agenda today."

These aren't long, involved statements, just short messages of appreciation and thanks. They take only a moment or two of your time, but can remain with the recipient for a lifetime. Try to communicate the appreciation you feel inside. It will be worth your effort.

Sharing Compliments

Everyone appreciates a compliment. During the course of your group work, you can compliment someone's effort, achievements, and character.

Complimenting effort.   One area we neglect to compliment others on is effort. We usually reserve our compliments for those moments when the first-place trophy is awarded, when the final problem is solved, or when the last obstacle is overcome. But those moments are few and far between. We need to notice and compliment the effort our fellow group members are putting forth right now, long before any problem is solved or any trophies are awarded. A simple statement complimenting someone's effort can really encourage an individual who may feel his efforts are going unnoticed. Compliment a person's efforts and you'll take another step toward building a cohesive group. You might make a friend, too!

Complimenting achievement.   Whenever a group member achieves some task or personal goal, verbally compliment the individual in front of the group (and personally after the meeting). Public complimenting of task or personal achievements builds solidarity and goodwill within the group. It communicates an unselfish, appreciative attitude on your part, and models complimentary behavior to other group members. Remember, your own behavior can have a ripple effect on the entire group. Compliment the achievement of others. It's amazing how productive a group can be when its members applaud the achievements of one another.

Complimenting character.   Who a person is, not what they've achieved, can be the focus of your compliment. Honesty, integrity, patience, understanding, caring, kindness, compassion, and humor are just some of the components of character you may want to compliment.

Rarely are individuals complimented on their character strengths. They might not even be aware of a particular facet of their character until you bring it to their attention. Complimenting character publicly in the group can also serve to draw attention and focus to a certain kind of behavior or attitude you want reinforced within the group. Show your appreciation for them by complimenting their character.

FEELING SUPPORTED

A fourth way to build a cohesive group is to make the members feel supported. Often during our lives we may feel no one understands us, no one cares, and no one is there to lend a helping hand. I think we've all felt this way a time or two. Whether it's showing understanding for someone who is frustrated with a group task or experiencing the pain of a recent divorce, these acts of support can deepen the social dimension of a group. A problem-solving group can do a great deal to provide support for its members by communicating empathy, communicating caring, and giving assistance.

Communicating Empathy

Empathy is the ability to feel what someone else is experiencing. This doesn't mean you need to assist, correct, or rescue the other person. It means you can understand or feel what the other person is feeling. An empathic response is often the only thing an individual wants—to feel someone understands. No desire for evaluation, advice, or even assistance. Just someone who understands.

Earlier we discussed listening for the speaker's feelings and ways to reflect those feelings back to the speaker. This is the primary way you can demonstrate empathy—to mirror feelings.

If you feel a group member could use the support that empathy provides, try listening for that person's emotional messages. Listen to how he or she might be feeling. Then reflect those feelings with active listening: "Sounds like you're really frustrated about…," "You're feeling upset about…," or "Sounds as if you're really happy about…."

Merely reflecting what you think the speaker is feeling and experiencing is a powerful way to demonstrate empathy. Notice that some of the statements dealt with positive feelings also. Empathy involves both positive and negative feelings. So be open and sensitive to reflecting both. Let them feel understood.

Communicating Caring

The second way you can communicate support to a group member is to tell them so. Once you understand what an individual is experiencing and you've demonstrated empathy, you can go the next step and communicate your concern. Nothing heavy. Just a word or two expressing concern or caring. Statements of caring and support can be very encouraging and uplifting. Here are some ways to communicate this form of support: "I hope things work out for you...," "I know you'll be fine...," and "I support your decision to...."

When a fellow group member experiences frustration with a task, conflict with another member, or falls behind on his group assignment, a word of encouragement or concern can make a difference in his attitude and resolve. We all need to know others care about what is going on with us. A brief sentence or two communicating caring can raise the spirits of a disappointed or discouraged individual.

Giving Assistance

In addition to demonstrating empathy and communicating caring, you should offer your assistance to other group members if you have an inclination to help and are in a position to do so. Most of the time such assistance will include making a copy of a report, helping with the overhead projector, or distributing written material. Sometimes your assistance might require more involvement, such as making a visual aid, typing a report, or giving a ride to the airport.

Take the opportunity to lend a helping hand. I know you have a million things to do yourself, but your assistance can be of tremendous support to another member and will nurture a cooperative spirit within the group. Don't be selfish with your time and energy if you see an opportunity to lend some help. The recipient of your help will remember your gesture, and the relationship between the two of you will be changed for the better.

Someone once said, "The purpose of life is to help others make it through." You can make the problem-solving group experience truly meaningful and significant if you help others. Your willingness to put your caring into action will do more to improve cohesion and commitment toward one another than any other act I know. It proves your support.

TRUSTING OTHERS

Although a person may feel included, acknowledged, valued, and supported in a group, the experience can be diluted and even negated if he or she senses an intentional manipulation or deception.

A furniture salesman can make us feel acknowledged and included. In fact, he can compliment, praise, and flatter us with expert mastery, but deep down we realize this is his job. He wants to manipulate and control us. To sell us. To get something from us. But in the end, do we really believe his compliments, warmth, and friendliness? Most likely not.

For the social dimension of a problem-solving group to achieve true cohesiveness, group members must trust one another. We need to trust that what they're saying is honest and true. We need to trust that their support and assistance are sincere. We need to trust that their warmth and friendship are genuine and heartfelt. Without this trust, all the other components necessary to building a cohesive group are suspect.

What indicators of trustworthiness are there? What clues can we search for in determining the level of trust we can give a particular individual? How do we know we can believe what someone is telling us?

The answer is we can't. No one can measure or predict with 100 percent accuracy the truthfulness of another individual's statement or behavior. There are no fail-proof tests, no totally accurate examinations. The best we can do is to assign probabilities to another person's honesty based on our past experiences with this individual. Oftentimes we are 99.99 percent certain that a person's statements are true or his behavior is sincerely motivated. But we are occasionally shocked by that 0.01 percent of the time when our predictions are wrong, and a trusted friend, colleague, or acquaintance lies or behaves in a dishonest way.

For the group to experience a high degree of cohesiveness, they must have a certain level of trust in one another. A basic trust that what an individual member says is true. That behavior accurately portrays his or her internal feelings and intentions. Without this trust, there can be no extended cooperation within the group, because communication would be doubted and behavior would be suspect.

Although there are no fail-proof tests for trusting others, there are two things you can ask to improve your decision to trust a certain individual. Does that person keep his or her word? How does that person treat others?

Does That Person Keep His Word?

Does an individual arrive at meetings on time? Can he keep his promise to show up on time or even show up at all? Does he complete assigned tasks? Or does he make up excuses or blame others for failure to finish a job? When someone makes you a promise to do something, does he actually follow through and make good on the promise? After a time, do you continue to believe or do you disregard his commitments to you?

If an individual keeps his word, you should be more likely to believe what he says is true. This doesn't work all the time. And there are exceptions to every rule. But a person who keeps promises is a better risk, as far as trusting is concerned, than someone who does not keep promises. Who keeps promises in your group?

How Does That Person Treat Others?

An individual's conduct with others is important to observe when determining whether to trust or distrust someone. How does this individual treat others? Does she gossip about others when the target of the gossip is absent? Does she lie or exaggerate the truth when she communicates with others? Do you sense manipulation or calculation in her actions and dealings with others? Is she inordinately complimentary or flattering to others in the group? In general, do you trust the way she treats others?

These two methods for determining the trustworthiness of an individual are helpful; but in the end, you must decide for yourself. For the purposes of decision-making and problem-solving in small groups, I assume the best and trust each group member will participate in an open, honest, and responsible manner. From this frame of reference, I can begin the group experience positively and optimistically.

GROUPTHINK: WHEN GROUPS ARE TOO COHESIVE

Making group members feel successful, included, acknowledged, supported, and trusted are five ingredients that make group members feel committed and dedicated to one another. The social climate of the group will determine its task effectiveness. And it is the social dimension experience that lives on in the memories and hearts of group members long after the task has been completed.

But you need to be careful that your group does not become too cohesive. The primary threat to sound decision-making and problem-solving with a group that experiences extreme cohesiveness is a phenomenon called groupthink.

Sociologist Irving Janis (1973) coined the term *groupthink* to describe the situation when a group departs from rational, reality-based decision-making to irrational, nonreality-based decision-making, because they are too cohesive. We will examine five conditions that can lead to groupthink, three symptoms of groupthink, and four ways to prevent groupthink.

Five Conditions That Can Lead to Groupthink

There are five conditions that can lead to groupthink. First, the group reaches an extremely high level of cohesiveness. Second, there's a shared perception among its members that the group can do no wrong. Third, the group is isolated from the contradictory input or feedback from individuals outside the group. Fourth, dissension within the group is prohibited. And finally, a lack of impartial leadership discourages group members from critically testing the evidence and reasoning of the group.

Three Symptoms of Groupthink

The first symptom of groupthink is when the group believes it is invulnerable and no harm can come to it. This perception is not based in reality, but is due to the extreme cohesiveness of the group. Once the group perceives itself as invulnerable, its decisions can involve more risk than the group would normally accept. The second symptom is pressure toward conformity. Dissension is discouraged and the group moves toward the majority view. Even if their ideas and proposals appear extreme to the group members themselves, they feel morally justified to pursue their objectives. Closed-mindedness is the third and final symptom of groupthink. The group will rationalize its decisions, even when the evidence points to contrary conclusions or a group member raises objections to their course of action.

It's important for you to be aware of these symptoms of groupthink and occasionally measure the behavior of your group against them. Does your group think no harm can come to it? Does it pressure its members toward conformity? And is it closed-minded?

If you answer yes to any of these questions, you need to consider the extent to which it is true. Simply because a group is occasionally closed-minded does not necessarily mean it is experiencing groupthink. But if your group experiences some of these symptoms for an extended period of time, you would be wise to bring them to the group's attention.

Four Ways to Prevent Groupthink

The best way to avoid groupthink is to take precautionary steps. It's much better to avoid the development of groupthink from the beginning than attempt to eliminate it once it's established. Here are four ways you can prevent groupthink from developing in your group.

1. Leader should stress critical evaluation.   From the very first meeting, the group leader should emphasize the role each group member is required to play in critically evaluating and analyzing the decision-making process of the group.

2. Seek outside feedback.   Each group member should discuss the decision-making processes with trusted colleagues outside the group and report these "outside" perceptions with the group.

3. Assign a devil's advocate within the group.   The leader can assign one group member to play the role of devil's advocate to challenge the prevailing ideas and proposals of the majority. The role of devil's advocate should be given to a different group member for each meeting.

4. Invite outside observation.   The group can occasionally invite a qualified individual from outside to observe the decision-making process of the group.

Use these techniques to keep the decision-making process in your group open, subject to critical analysis, and reality based. Everything you do in your group affects each member in some way. A smile, a compliment, or an invitation for coffee can change a life. You might never fully realize your impact on the group members, but I would encourage you to discover the caring, sensitive, and loving aspects of who you are. Perhaps it will be in a problem-solving group that you discover many beautiful things about yourself.

This chapter examined five ways you can build a cohesive problem-solving group. When all group members experiences some level of success, connection, value, support, and trust, they will more likely experience a social dimension that produces a cohesive group. It is this cohesiveness that enhances their ability to solve the problems brought before them.

INDIVIDUAL AND GROUP EXERCISES

Exercise 9.1   Sharing Appreciation

Reflect on your personal life and notice the 80 percent that is working well. From the list of things in your life that are going smoothly, select one individual who is currently contributing to this process. Perhaps it's a friend who occasionally calls just to see how you're doing. Maybe it's a coworker who gave you a hand on a project the other day. And possibly your spouse was especially thoughtful or concerned this morning. After you've selected an individual who is contributing to your well-being, thank her with some home-baked cookies, a bouquet of flowers from your backyard, or a gift certificate to your favorite restaurant. Let this person know you appreciate her role in your life.

Exercise 9.2   Devil's Advocate in the Group

Have your group attempt to solve a mini-problem, and once the group begins to reach consensus on a proposed solution, have one of the members play the role of devil's advocate. The role-player should question the reasoning and opinions of the majority membership. The devil's advocate should raise objections to the proposed solution and continue to object for at least 10 minutes. How did the devil's advocate influence the group? How did the role-player feel? What positive contributions to group problem-solving can a devil's advocate have on the group process?

T E N
MANAGING CONFLICT

No fight. No blame.
–Lao Tsu

The refrigerator light cast a white glow on the two young boys as they sat on the kitchen floor, bickering with one another.

Between the two brothers was a plate containing the last slice of apple pie, which they were going to share. Holding the butter knife in one hand, the seven-year-old was trying to cut the piece in two, while the younger brother was grabbing at the knife, complaining he always got the smaller piece when his brother was in charge of dividing the remains of a dessert. Back and forth they bickered as they tugged on the butter knife. Then their mom entered the scene of the conflict.

"What are you kids fighting about now?" asked the mother.

"When Tyler cuts the pie, he always gives me the smallest piece," complained the younger brother.

"I do not," Tyler shot back.

"You do too," yelled Jared.

"Do not."

"Do too."

"Okay, you guys. Settle down. I've got an idea," suggested the mom. "How about one of you cuts the pie and the other gets to select the first piece."

Smiles slowly broke out on both the young boys' faces.

"All right, I'll still cut the pie," said Tyler. And he did. But Tyler never measured, eyed, and remeasured a piece of pie so carefully as he did this one, because he knew Jared got to choose. So he cut the piece perfectly in half.

Jared got to select the piece he wanted, but Tyler didn't mind because each piece was exactly the same size. Both parties agreed to a solution they found acceptable. The conflict was peacefully resolved, but it wouldn't be the last before they went to sleep.

"And shut that refrigerator door!" the mom said as she winked at the boys.

A DIFFERENT APPROACH TO CONFLICT

The mother could have settled this conflict in many ways. She could have ignored the battle and walked past the skirmish. She could have punished both boys for fighting. She could have eaten the pie herself to teach the boys a lesson.

But she didn't. She flowed with their conflict. She joined with their little clash and suggested an alternative that required their cooperation and produced an acceptable solution they were both happy with. If only the rest of our conflicts could be so easily resolved.

In your small group work, you and the other members will occasionally experience conflict. A struggle over the placement of an item on the agenda. An argument over the merits of a proposed solution. Or feuding between two members of the group. These and other situations can reduce the group's task effectiveness and strain the relationships of its members.

Group members can ignore or deny conflict. They can address it indirectly through innuendo and insinuation. They can be more direct and blame and punish. They can even expel the member causing conflict. They, like the mother of the two boys, have many methods at their disposal for dealing with conflict.

Problem-solving groups often employ counterproductive approaches in dealing with conflict. They close their eyes. They blame. They hit. And they hurt. Yet such approaches do very little to resolve conflict. And in many instances they serve to escalate differences, increase tension, and sever relationships within the group.

There's an old Zen saying that suggests another approach to dealing with conflict: "Hug your problem and it may disappear." This might sound paradoxical. Hug your problem? Aren't we trained to run from conflict? Or at least find someone to blame for the mess to distance us from responsibility? "It's not my fault," we say.

I think the "hugging" suggestion is actually an invitation to get closer to conflict rather than further away. It suggests a direct and open exploration of conflict, without blame or punishment. Conflict can be a wonderful teacher. It can teach us valuable lessons about others and ourselves. Instead of always trying to ignore, deny, blame, or fight during conflict, we can choose to join with it. Acknowledge its presence openly in the group. Explore rather than blame. Loosen rather than tighten. We need to flow with our conflict.

This chapter will explore the topic of group conflict. We will look at the myths of conflict, the advantages of conflict, three types of conflict experienced within groups, and strategies to address the various types of conflict.

MYTHS OF CONFLICT

Before we discuss ways to manage conflict, let's define conflict and examine some of its myths and advantages. *Conflict* is a struggle or disagreement between two or more options or people. This struggle or disagreement can be over differences of opinions, beliefs, or values in the task dimension of the group. Conflict can also be experienced in the social dimension between two or more people having differences in feelings, perceptions, and behaviors. I discuss three commonly held myths concerning conflict. They are conflict should be avoided at all cost, conflict is always someone else's fault, and all conflict can be resolved.

Myth 1: Avoid Conflict At All Costs

One of the most common ways to deal with conflict is to avoid it. Now this is good advice if you're walking down a dark alley and you see three figures lurking behind the garbage bins. You should turn and walk the other way. Sometimes conflict, or possible conflict, can and should be avoided.

But in your small group problem-solving efforts, don't avoid conflict at all costs. Conflict can often benefit the task and social dimensions of the group. In fact, conflict can be an opportunity to listen to differences, discover new common ground, and uncover more effective ways to interact together as a group. It's out of the differences of group members that strength is built and wiser decisions are made.

Myth 2: Conflict Is Always Someone Else's Fault

Frequently, our first response when conflict occurs is to find someone to blame. It's what I call the "Blame first, explore later" syndrome. We blame first, then we may examine what the problem really was. Many times we fail to explore the various factors of a disagreement or dispute. We want to blame. Maybe because if someone else is to blame, we can't be at fault. In the complexity of group work, there might not be someone at fault or someone to blame. Maybe we're barking up the wrong tree when we automatically look for a culprit rather than examine the disagreement at hand. Anytime you have five or six people working together, there will be, and should be, differences of opinion. When these differences surface, instead of finding someone to blame or fault, you may want to first explore and examine. Your group will function better when you do.

Myth 3: All Conflict Can Be Resolved

The final myth I would like to address is that all conflict can be resolved. The belief that if we try hard enough, if we talk long enough, and if we compromise well enough, we will eventually resolve whatever conflict is before us. This is not always the case.

Not all substantive or idea conflicts can be resolved in a manner acceptable to all parties. Especially those issues concerning questions of value. Conflicts centered on what is morally, ethically, and theologically correct and true might never be satisfactorily resolved in the group. Deep seeded personality conflicts between two group members might never be adequately resolved and healed during the life of the group.

Some conflicts might never be resolved. And that's okay. That's life. Not every relationship works. Not every dream is realized. Not every desire satisfied. Our lesson can be to learn to let go in situations like this, give in to another individual's wishes, accommodate others for the sake of the group. Not all conflict can be resolved. It might ultimately involve our departure from the group.

ADVANTAGES OF CONFLICT

Anytime conflict exists within a group, there is always the potential for growth for each group member. This growth can take the form of expanded awareness, improved participation, increased productivity, greater cohesiveness, and developed maturity.

Advantage 1: Expanded Awareness

Many times when a group is running smoothly, its members working together cooperatively, there is a sense of satisfaction, a feeling of well-being. Complacency can often result. And a deadening of the senses can occur, which may cause a trancelike state. If you've ever ridden on a train across flatland for an extended period of time, you know how quickly the monotony of the ride can lull you to sleep.

When conflict is brought out into the open it can have an arousing effect upon group members. They are awakened from the productive hum of their routines. They are called to process, interact, and behave in a different, more focused manner. They are now in the midst of a conflict! The shift in focus from the mundane to the exceptional can be stimulating. It can wake us from our sleep.

Advantage 2: Improved Participation

Just as the mere introduction of open conflict to the group process can foster expanded awareness, it can also encourage increased participation from group members. Many times, members will spring to action and participate with greater frequency and enthusiasm when the discussion turns to matters of dispute and struggle. In fact, many a relationship has been based upon this one variable— conflict.

Advantage 3: Increased Productivity

The results of disagreement over substantive and procedural conflicts can benefit the productivity of the group. When the group resolves conflict and discovers new solutions, ideas, and procedures, the productivity can be greater than before the conflict. The labor pains brought about by conflict might also signal the birth of fresh ideas, better solutions, and improved relationships.

Advantage 4: Greater Cohesiveness

After the group deals with interpersonal conflict in a productive and healthy manner, the cohesiveness of the group can be greatly enhanced. A better understanding and working relationship often results from interpersonal conflicts between group members if the group handles the conflict positively and maturely. Once the group members share perceptions, air differences, and establish new common ground for interacting and relating to one another, they can share more intimate feelings of connection.

Cohesion within the group frequently occurs when the group resolves substantive conflicts regarding the task dimension also. With the struggle over a specific task successfully negotiated and put behind them, the group can experience a feeling of achievement and intimacy. Good work often fosters good feelings.

Advantage 5: Developed Maturity

Conflict within a group can help an individual increase in maturity. By that I mean, grow up. Each one of us is childish and infantile in certain areas of our lives. And having to butt heads and hearts with other human beings in our group can provide us with a rich, growing environment from which we can develop our abilities to disengage our egos, practice empathy, exercise patience, demonstrate compromise, and ask for forgiveness. These and many other activities brought about by conflict can tremendously benefit our personal growth and development as human beings.

THREE TYPES OF GROUP CONFLICT

When you consider the enormous potential for conflict within any problem-solving group, it's amazing any collection of individuals can work together in relative harmony and reach agreement on any matter. Literally thousands upon thousands of minor and major task and social dimension issues can ignite disagreement and struggle.

Every group experiences conflicts. Each conflict centers on a different issue. Each conflict focuses on differences, yet requires distinctly unique perceptions, approaches, and interventions on the part of group members to address the conflict successfully. No matter what conflict you face, it will fall into one of three categories: procedural conflict, substantive conflict, and interpersonal conflict. Let's briefly define each of these.

Procedural Conflict (Structure)

A *procedural conflict* deals with the structure or procedures the group follows during discussion. These procedures outline how the meeting will be run, the order of the agenda, how disagreement will be handled, and how decisions will be made. A procedural conflict involves disagreement or struggle over the mechanics of the group's operation.

Substantive Conflict (Issues)

A *substantive conflict* involves disagreement or struggle over the substance or issues of discussion. This type of conflict centers around the task dimension of the group. Substantive conflict can involve disagreement or arguments over the tests of evidence, analysis of reasoning, the debate over proposed solutions, or any matter that deals with the content of discussion. Whereas a procedural conflict debates the mechanics of how something will be done or conducted within the group, a substantive conflict struggles with the ideas, opinions, beliefs, and values of group members themselves.

Interpersonal Conflict (People)

Tension or conflict between individual members of the group is called *interpersonal conflict* because it involves the feelings and behaviors of individuals. Although interpersonal conflict can often present itself as a procedural or substantive conflict initially, stronger feelings and statements attacking the person (ad hominem attack) can result, unmasking conflict between people.

Now that you know the basic differences between procedural, substantive, and interpersonal conflicts, I'll present some specific ways to deal with each category of conflict.

DEALING WITH PROCEDURAL CONFLICT

Any conflict or struggle aimed at the process or method by which the group works is called a procedural conflict. These types of conflicts often involve:

- Changes in the frequency, times, and locations of meetings
- Changes in the agenda format
- Changes in the structure of the meeting itself
- Extending debate on a controversial issue
- Terminating debate on a controversial issue
- Modification of decision-making procedures
- Modification of speaking rights/time limits

How to Resolve Procedural Conflict

The group leader or chairperson needs to identify these conflicts, bring them to the group's attention, and act on them. Normally, the leader will have the power to accept or reject a proposed change in the procedures of the group. And the leader's decision is final.

But if there is no designated leader, or the leader wants to employ a more democratic method for discussing and structuring the procedures of the group, the leader can adopt a more open process. This process involves the basic parliamentary procedure steps:

1. Have a proposal (motion) stated to the group.
2. Ask if there is a second (a second member supporting the motion).
3. If there isn't a second, the proposal is rejected.
4. If there is a second, the group discusses the proposal.
5. A vote is taken when the discussion is completed.
6. The proposal is either accepted or rejected based upon the vote.

I prefer this method when faced with a procedural conflict because it directs the question back to group members, it opens discussion to all, and the decision is based on the majority vote. If the majority of the group votes to accept or reject the proposal, there is usually majority support to enforce the old or new procedure.

DEALING WITH SUBSTANTIVE CONFLICT

The second category of conflict experienced in groups involves ideas and issues. The focus of substantive conflict is what the group is discussing, not how it is being discussed. These content issues can include disagreement concerning the:

- Reliability of information or evidence
- Reasoning supporting a proposal or idea
- Acceptability of an opinion or idea
- Acceptability of a specific proposal
- Acceptability of a goal or objective of the group

When a group experiences substantive conflict, the leader or the group might attempt to resolve the conflict by avoidance. The group can drop the issue and move to another topic. The leader can force a decision upon group members, thus eliminating the substantive debate. The leader or group can also try to please members of both sides by using compromise and having both sides give a little ground. Finally, the group can vote to determine what idea will prevail. Each strategy for dealing with substantive conflict reduces the group's effectiveness by prematurely eliminating open and honest discussion of the issue, forcing compromise, and imposing a win-lose atmosphere on the group's social dimension.

How to Resolve Substantive Conflict

An open discussion of the issue is required with all substantive conflict. Whether group members vigorously debate the admissibility of evidence to the discussion and the reasoning of a proposal, or modify the primary purpose of the group, these guidelines will contribute to a more positive, productive, and successful approach to substantive conflict:

1. Identify the conflict.   State the substantive conflict in specific terms. Summarize the differences of opinion or sides to the debate.

2. Share perceptions.   Once you've brought the conflict out for discussion, ask the other members for their perceptions of the conflict and the seriousness of the conflict.

3. Share opinions.   Group members can voice their opinions about the issue, but should refrain from verbally attacking members with the opposing viewpoint. Remind the group that it's possible to disagree with another person without having to dislike him or her. Focus on issues, not personalities.

4. Listen actively.   Whenever an individual has made a statement, have the opposition restate the idea or feeling to the satisfaction of the speaker. This listening for understanding will promote more accurate communication and prevent emotions from escalating during discussion.

5. State opposition's strengths.   Have the opposing sides point out the strengths in the other's arguments or opinions. This is the difficult one. They won't normally want to state the other's strengths, but if you can get them to participate in this fifth step, you've come a long way to bringing about agreement.

6. Discover common ground.   Try to have the opposing sides discover something they can both agree on. It doesn't necessarily have to be a major point of agreement—just some common ground both sides can agree to. Perhaps both sides can only agree that a conflict exists and they will work to resolve the conflict. That's a beginning. From this point of common ground, the two sides can hopefully discover more points of agreement as the discussion continues.

7. Take a break.   After heated and often draining debate, a break is in order for the group. Take a five- or 10-minute break to stretch the legs, talk about something else, and get something to drink.

8. Continue the discussion or move on. After the break, continue the process of Steps 3 to 6 until the sides reach some sort of consensus on how they see the issue, proposal, or group goal. Or, after extended discussion, the group might feel that no common ground or consensus can be reached and will need to discuss how to move on despite difference of opinion. Remind the group of all the things that are working and going well, and that this particular issue is just one of many the group will face in its the life.

You probably recognized that this eight-step process is a modification of the consensus decision-making technique presented in Chapter 5. And it should be, because the purpose of consensus is to discover a proposal, decision, or solution to some problem (or conflict) that is workable and acceptable to all group members.

In your dealings with substantive conflicts, keep in mind that the reason we work in small groups is to utilize the best each member is willing and able to contribute to achieve the group's goal. Differences of ideas will inevitably surface, but those differences also constitute the strength of the discussion process. It's the discarding of those ideas the group decides are unnecessary and the retaining of those ideas it feels are valuable that makes the group's product superior to the best individual's product.

DEALING WITH INTERPERSONAL CONFLICT

Sometimes there might be conflict between two group members. The interpersonal conflict can be minor and fleeting. Examples of this are inappropriate remarks directed at an individual or a rude comment spoken in frustration, where in each instance, someone was upset or hurt by the comment. The interpersonal conflict can also be major and sustained, as in the case of aggressive and open feuding between two or more group members. Here are some causes of interpersonal conflict:

- Residual emotional injury from substantive or procedural conflict
- Different values and beliefs
- Cultural or racial differences
- Different personalities
- Different communication styles (dysfunctional roles)

No matter what causes the interpersonal conflict, it negatively affects the social dimension of the group because one or more members experience conflict at the personal level with another individual or individuals within the group.

Often interpersonal conflict can be disguised or presented as a procedural or substantive conflict, but the real cause of the dispute is a concealed interpersonal conflict between two or more members. Even during legitimate procedural or substantive conflicts, tempers may flair and feelings get hurt, which can invite retaliation and attack at the personal level. It's often difficult to prevent sustained substantive conflict from developing into interpersonal conflict. Our hearts are connected to our heads in ways we don't yet fully understand.

How to Resolve Interpersonal Conflict Caused by Dysfunctional Behavior

The controller, blamer, pleaser, distractor, and ghost presented in Chapter 3 are dysfunctional communication patterns. If you suspect the individual with whom you are having interpersonal problems fits one of these five dysfunctional role descriptions, refer to Chapter 7 for specific interventions you can use to address the situation. Keep in mind that you should bring severe dysfunctional behavior exhibited by a group member to the attention of the group leader who should take appropriate action. If the interventions suggested in Chapter 7 do not accomplish the goals of the group, then the leader might seek professional help.

How to Resolve Interpersonal Conflict Caused by Normal Differences

Now the good news. The majority of your conflict with others in a group will not involve individuals exhibiting dysfunctional behavior. Most of your interpersonal conflict in the group can be dealt with using the guidelines suggested here:

1. Self-check-in.   Before you do anything, just sit and breathe. Don't say anything to the individual you're experiencing difficulty with. Just sit and breathe for now. After the meeting, go home and conduct a five-minute check-in with yourself about this conflict. Ask yourself, What specifically did this individual say or do to upset me? Did I overreact? Am I overly sensitive today? How am I doing in other aspects of my life? Am I still upset about what this person said or did? Before you do anything, sleep on it. Do you feel the same after you awaken? If you're feeling better, good. Give the individual another chance. If not, go to Step 2.

2. Ask for third-person perception check.   Share your perception and discuss this matter with another group member who is
not involved in the conflict. Briefly share your basic perceptions of
the conflict, then ask this third party for her perceptions of the remark, behavior, or event. Did that person share your perceptions? If
not, consider the feedback of this individual and put the matter on
hold for a while. If the conflict recurs, then start over at Step 1. If the
third party confirms your perceptions, go to Step 3.

3. Decide what you want.   Once you've received some confir-
mation from a third party regarding the conflict, decide what you
want to do. Do you want to let the incident go? Do you want to share
your perceptions with the individual? Do you want to retaliate in
kind? Do you want to punish the person? Do you want an apology?
What do you really want? Think long and hard about his one. Most
of the time, if the conflict was a brief, one-time event (a remark, a
joke, an accusation, a slur), you'll let it go and see if it happens
again. If you won't let it go, don't consider retaliation, punishment,
or even getting an apology. Go to Step 4.

4. Conduct perception check-in with the individual.   Ask the
individual if you can meet for two or three minutes after the next
meeting. If she asks what you want to discuss, explain that you want
to share your perceptions of a recent event involving her. If she
refuses, let it go. Then go back to Step 1. Don't push the matter. If
you can meet, ask for her perceptions of the event. In most instances, the individual will either defend the behavior, back off and modify her position, or apologize. If she apologizes, accept the apology,
shake hands, and let go of it. If the person backs off and modifies
her position, support that position in whatever way you're comfortable and go to Step 5. If the person attacks you, disagrees with your
perception, or defends her position, remain calm and breathe. Then
go to Step 5.

5. State your boundary.   A boundary is an imaginary line that
separates what is acceptable to you from what is *not* acceptable to
you. If the individual disagreed with your perception, defended or
modified her position, you need to state your boundary regarding
future behavior. A boundary statement is not a blaming, accusing, or
punishing statement. It is an informational statement. It's basic structure is: If you _____, then I am prepared to _____.

6. Enforce your boundary statement.   The very next time the individual repeats the unacceptable behavior, enforce your boundary response. Whether that means identifying the interaction, leaving the meeting room, or bringing the matter to the attention of the group, you enforce your boundary statement, immediately.

This six-step interpersonal conflict resolution model is just that, a model. It's one way to manage interpersonal conflict. There are other methods you might want to learn about in the future, but this approach is simple and direct. Regardless of your strategy, however, remember that a gentle, open, and sincere attitude on your part will help create an atmosphere where you can invite the other into dialogue.

FORGIVENESS

To conclude this chapter I'd like to discuss a subject that lies at the foundation of your work with others in small groups, especially in the area of conflict, and that topic is forgiveness. *Forgiveness* is the act of granting free pardon for an offense. In essence, it is the act of letting go of the desire to get even, to make someone pay for the hurt he or she might have caused you during some disagreement or conflict. It is also the act of asking someone to forgive you for an offense you might have caused them.

In any group process, people's efforts will often fall short, circumstances will not always accommodate the best-laid plans, and your feelings and those of your group members will eventually be hurt by some incidental or catastrophic event. When we are hurt by someone, be it a critical remark or an act of betrayal, we experience the initial feeling of shock, dismay, or a host of other uncomfortable feelings. But eventually, each of these feelings gives rise to anger. The anger of being injured by another individual. When we are hurt, we ultimately experience anger. One of two things can be done with this anger. We can hold on to the anger or let go of it. We will explore ways to let go.

When we hurt another person, guilt is most often the resulting feeling we must live with. Guilt for a remark made in anger, an expectation we cannot live up to, or an act of deception. No matter what we did to bring pain to another person, guilt is our eventual destination if we don't make amends with the one we hurt.

Whether we are prisoners of our anger or prisoners of our guilt, we are held hostage by these powerful feelings until we decide to let go of them. And the only way I know to be free from their suffocating grasp is the act of forgiveness. But to forgive and to ask for forgiveness requires an abandonment of your usual, familiar way of dealing with hurt, anger, and guilt. Here are three principles of forgiveness that will help you when attempting to let go instead of getting even—forgiveness is a decision not a feeling, forgiveness requires suspension of your ego, and forgiveness is a never-ending process.

1. Forgiveness is a decision, not a feeling.   An erroneous concept regarding forgiveness is that you should feel like forgiving someone before you communicate your forgiveness of their offense. Forgiveness has nothing to do with your feelings. Forgiveness is a decision to consciously let go of your guilt or anger. Initially, forgiveness has more to do with your head than your heart. Don't use the excuse that you don't feel like asking for forgiveness or forgiving someone for an offense. Forgiveness is not a feeling, it is a decision.

2. Forgiveness requires suspension of the ego.   As I stated earlier, your decision to forgive or ask for forgiveness is a difficult task. It requires that you suspend your ego—putting yourself second. This is not an easy process—to occasionally suspend our preoccupation with ourselves. Yet it is essential to the act of forgiveness.

3. Forgiveness is a never-ending process.   Whether we have made the decision to ask for forgiveness or grant forgiveness, the process of forgiving is a never-ending task. Forgiving is not a destination. Rather it is a way of traveling. It is actually something we become over time—a forgiving individual. Forgiving demands of us the greatest of all tasks: the willingness we permit others, and ourselves, to make mistakes.

Asking for Forgiveness

The first type of forgiveness we will examine is the forgiveness we ask of others. If you have wronged someone in your group and want to ask their forgiveness, you might want to try the AAA Forgiveness Technique. It involves the following three steps:

1. **A**dmit you were wrong.
2. **A**pologize for the offense.
3. **A**sk their forgiveness.

Let's assume you criticized another group member unfairly during a meeting. The following day you feel guilty about your critical remarks. You decide to ask the individual for forgiveness. This is how the AAA Forgiveness Technique works:

You: Nathan, do you remember the meeting last Thursday?
Nathan: I've been trying to forget.
You: *Well, I was wrong to criticize you in front of the group.* (admitting you were wrong)
Nathan: You bet you were. That was a terrible thing to do. Would I ever do something like that to you?
You: No. Probably not. But *I apologize for criticizing you. I'm sorry.* (apologizing for the offense)
Nathan: Apology accepted, I guess.
You: *Would you forgive me for criticizing you?* (asking for forgiveness)
Nathan: Well, yes. Of course I'll forgive you.

Not all attempts at asking someone for forgiveness will go this smoothly. But did you notice how you admitted you were wrong, apologized for the offense, and asked for forgiveness? This AAA Forgiveness Technique can be very useful in dealing with your guilt over something you have done. It can bring you to a place of forgiveness and that's one of the nicest things you can do for yourself. Remember—be gentle on yourself.

Forgiving Others

The second area of forgiveness we'll examine is forgiving others. When someone has hurt or offended you, your initial response will range from mild surprise to rage. Eventually, your hurt will turn to anger. What you do with this anger will determine, to a large extent, the kind of person you will become and the quality of all your relationships. If you choose to hold on to the anger, you will become bitter. And this bitterness can affect every area of your relational life.

There are two specific instances we will explore. The first instance is where the individual is not apologetic for the pain he has caused you. The second case is where the person apologizes and asks your forgiveness. No matter which of the two responses the other individual chooses, your work is to forgive them.

Forgiving those who are not apologetic.   There will be occasions when someone hurts you and is not apologetic, let alone repentant enough to ask you for forgiveness. In this instance, you might forgive them anyway.

You might not want to forgive him initially. In fact, you might never feel the desire to forgive him for the wrong he has done you. But forgiveness is not a feeling. It's your decision to be free of the hurt and anger he has brought you. You can use three methods to forgive those who have hurt you and refuse to be apologetic.

The first method I refer to as *pretending to forgive*. It can be used when the hurt is too recent or too serious for you to even consider a decision to forgive the other person. Here's how the technique works. You place two chairs about three feet apart, facing one another. You sit in one chair and imagine the person who hurt you in the empty chair. Next, you pretend you have decided to forgive this person (even though you have not really made this decision) and you tell the "other person" in the empty chair you have forgiven the offense. Picture the other person's face softening as you say the words. Imagine the other person saying something thoughtful, considerate, or even apologetic. After you have told the person you have forgiven her, just sit in your chair and feel your response to the exercise. Do you feel the same? Do you feel a slight change? Do you still feel the hurt or anger?

The second method in dealing with those who are not apologetic is a technique I call *imagining their death*. The technique involves you imagining the person has only one day to live. Even though this individual is healthy, happy, and still not apologetic, you are to imagine that person has only 24 hours to live. In 24 hours the person will be dead. Do you feel the same? Do you feel slightly different? Do you still focus on your hurt? Or are you thinking about the other person? Have your feelings changed about the relative importance of her offense compared to her impending death? You'd be surprised how this will change your feelings toward the person.

The third technique is what I call *direct forgiving*. After you have decided to forgive the other person for his offense, you share this information with him in person, face-to-face. The primary weakness to this method is that the other person will often respond with denial, justification, rationalization, or blame. He might even deny he did in fact offend you. No matter what response he chooses, you emphasize the fact that you have chosen to forgive him for his offense. You don't have to be the best of friends after the meeting. The single purpose for the meeting is for you to let him know you have forgiven him.

Forgiving those who ask for your forgiveness.   If someone who has hurt you comes to you and asks for your forgiveness you should forgive her, no matter how you feel. Remember forgiveness is not a feeling, but a decision. You need to forgive her if you are to be free. If you decide not to forgive, you, not the other person, will carry the weight of anger and resentment.

Forgive those who ask for forgiveness. It's really the only choice you have if you want to be free. Forgiveness may be the most important lesson you'll learn while you participate in and lead small groups.

This chapter examined three types of conflict—procedural, substantive, and interpersonal. It outlined various ways these types of conflict can manifest themselves and suggested a number of approaches to each kind of conflict. If conflict should arise in your problem-solving group, keep in mind that conflict is natural in any setting where individuals feel free to express their opinions. Conflict should not be avoided, but rather, it should be explored so better solutions to problems can be generated, and healthier, more cooperative group participation be encouraged. Finally, forgiveness was examined as a powerful method for remaining free of anger and guilt when working with others in small groups.

INDIVIDUAL AND GROUP EXERCISES

Exercise 10.1   Boundary Making

Communicate a boundary to an individual whose behavior is unacceptable to you. Select someone from your personal life (spouse, parent, child, best friend, or acquaintance) or professional life (coworkers, supervisor, or employee) who did or said something that bothered you. Arrange a two- or three-minute meeting with this individual and share your boundary with her. Complete this premeeting form before you meet with this person.

1. Who is this individual? _____

2. What behavior is unacceptable to you? _____

3. Construct your boundary statement.

   If you _____.

   I am prepared to _____.

When you share your boundary with this person, provide some brief introductory remarks about the situation before you communicate your boundary. The purpose of the meeting is not to blame or punish, but rather to inform the individual what you find unacceptable and what you are prepared to do if the behavior is repeated.

How did your meeting go? How did you feel composing your boundary statement? How did you feel asking this person for a meeting? How did you feel communicating your boundary to this individual? How did the person respond? Have you noticed a change in the person's behavior since your meeting? How can you incorporate boundary making into your small group?

Exercise 10.2   Group Conflict Resolution

Have your group use some of the procedures outlined in this chapter the next time it experiences either a procedural or substantive conflict. Assign one group member to identify any procedural conflict the group experiences and act as the facilitator to resolve the conflict. Assign another group member to identify any substantive conflict and facilitate the group's interactions during that conflict.

AFTERWORD

What lies behind us and what lies before us
are tiny matters compared to what lies within us.
–Emerson

Several years ago I conducted a series of communications work-shops for telephone operators at Pacific Bell Telephone. One of the workshop activities required each participant to lead his or her group in a problem-solving task for 10 minutes using the guiding behaviors presented in Chapter 7.

At the end of a morning workshop, one of the participants approached me and said, "I've never led a group before today and I actually liked it."

"Maybe you should go into management," I responded, half jok-ingly.

"No, I can't see myself leading meetings," she said. "Anyway, I like being an operator."

"But maybe you might give some thought to leading others," I encouraged her in a more serious tone.

"Well, I've never thought of myself as a manager," she said after a few moments, "but I did like guiding my group during the work-shop."

"Who knows," I said, "the next time I conduct a training session here, you might be the person in charge."

We both laughed and said our good-byes.

Less than a year later, I received a letter from that same woman telling me she had completed her first class at a local community college, marking the beginning of her studies in Personnel Manage-ment. She concluded her note with these words: "I never knew I had a desire to lead groups until we did that activity in your workshop last spring. Thanks for helping me see the leader inside me."

When you began reading this book, you may have had little or no experience in leading a problem-solving group. But as the title of the book suggests, within you is the ability to become a leader. Not only can you become an effective group member, you can also lead the same group. It doesn't matter who you were or where you were headed, within you is a leader—one who helps a group reach its goal.

I encourage you, after reading this book, to discover the leader within you. Whether you eventually command a multinational corporation or coordinate a family reunion, the skills you have learned will enable you to run a small group effectively and help that group achieve its goals. When the opportunity presents itself, I hope you will allow the leader within you to come forward.

BIBLIOGRAPHY

Chapter 1. Working in a Group

Bales, R. 1976. *Interaction Process Analysis.* Chicago: University of Chicago Press.

Fisher, A. 1970. "Decision Emergence: Phases in Group Decision Making" *Speech Monographs* 37:53–66.

Fisher, A. and Ellis, D. 1990. *Small Group Communication: Communication and Process.* New York: McGraw-Hill.

Hirokawa, R. Y. and Poole, M. 1986. *Communication and Group Decision-Making.* Beverly Hills, Calif.: Sage Publications.

Poole, M. S. 1981. "Decision Development in Small Groups I: A Comparison of Two Models." *Communication Monographs* 48:1–17.

Shaw, M. 1981. *Group Dynamics: The Psychology of Small Group Behavior.* New York: McGraw-Hill.

Chapter 2. Discovering Yourself

Adler, R. and Towne, N. 1995. *Looking Out, Looking In.* Orlando, Fla.: Holt, Rinehart, and Winston

Moore, T. 1992. *Care of the Soul.* New York: HarperCollins.

Stevens, J. O. 1990. *Awareness: Exploring, Experimenting, Experiencing.* New York: Bantam.

Storr, A. 1993. *Solitude.* New York: Free Press.

Chapter 3. Speaking Clearly

Hayakawa, S. I. 1964. *Language in Thought and Action.* New York: Harcourt Brace Jovanovich.

Satir, V. 1988. *New Peoplemaking.* New York: Science and Behavior.

Tannen, D. 1986. *That's Not What I Meant!* New York: Morrow.

Chapter 4. Listening for Understanding

Axline, V. 1967. *Dibs: In Search of Self.* New York: Ballantine Books.

Floyd, J. 1985. *Listening: A Practical Approach*. Glenview, Ill.: Scott, Foresman.

Gordon, T. 1970. *Parent Effectiveness Training*. New York: Wyden.

Chapter 5.   Problem-Solving in Groups

Bormann, E. G. 1990. *Small Group Communication: Theory and Practice*. New York: Harper and Row.

Dewey, J. 1910. *How We Think*. Boston: D.C. Heath.

Gouran, D. S. 1991. "Rational Approaches to Decision-Making and Problem-Solving Discussion." *Quarterly Journal of Speech* 77:343–358.

Hall, J. and Watson, W. 1970. "The Effects of a Normative Intervention on Group Decision-Making." *Human Relations*: 23:299-317.

Hirokawa, R. Y. 1985. "Discussion Procedures and Decision-Making Performance: A Test of a Functional Perspective." *Human Communication Research* 12:203-224.

———. 1988. "A Descriptive Investigation into the Possible Communication-Based Reasons for Effective and Ineffective Group Decision-Making." *Communication Monographs* 50:363-79.

Hirokawa, R.Y. and Poole, M. 1986. *Communication and Group Decision-Making*. Beverly Hills, Calif.: Sage Publications.

Poole, M. S. 1981. "Decision Development in Small Groups I: A Comparison of Two Models." *Communication Monographs* 48:1-17.

Schultz, B. 1996. *Communicating in the Small Group*. New York: HarperCollins.

von Oech, R. 1990. *A Whack on the Side of the Head*. New York: Warner Books.

Wood, J. et al. 1986. *Group Discussion: A Practical Guide to Participation and Leadership*. New York: Harper and Row.

Chapter 6.   Preparing for Discussion

Beebe, S. 1995. *Communicating in Small Groups: Principles and Practice*. New York: HarperCollins

Roszak, T. 1986. *The Cult of Information*. New York: Pantheon Books.

Wilson, G. and Hanna, M. 1993. *Groups in Context*. New York: McGraw-Hill.

Chapter 7.   Guiding Discussion

Benne, K. and Sheats, P. 1948. "Functional Roles of Group Members." *Journal of Social Issues* 4:41–49.

Dyer, W. G. 1972. *The Sensitive Manipulator.* Provo, Utah: Brigham Young University Press.

Johnson, D. 1987. *Joining Together: Group Theory and Group Skills.* Englewood Cliffs, N.J.: Prentice-Hall.

Chapter 8.   Leading a Group

Barge, J. K. 1994. *Leadership: Communication Skills for Organizations and Groups.* New York: St. Martin's Press.

Bass, B. 1985. *Leadership and Performance Beyond Expectations.* New York: Free Press.

Fiedler, F. 1967. *A Theory of Leadership Effectiveness.* New York: McGraw-Hill.

Schultz, B. 1996. *Communicating in the Small Group.* New York: HarperCollins.

Stogdill, R. M. 1974. *Handbook of Leadership.* New York: Free Press.

Wood, J. et al. 1986. *Group Discussion: A Practical Guide to Participation and Leadership.* New York: Harper and Row.

Chapter 9.   Building a Cohesive Group

Bormann, E. and Bormann, N. 1988. *Effective Small Group Communication.* Edina, Minn.: Burgess Publishing.

Fisher, B. and Ellis, D. 1990. *Small Group Decision Making: Communication and the Small Group Process.* New York: McGraw-Hill.

Janis, I. 1973. *Victims of Groupthink.* Boston: Houghton Mifflin.

————. 1983. *Groupthink: Psychological Studies of Policy Decisions and Fiascoes.* Boston: Houghton Mifflin.

Shaw, M. 1981. *Group Dynamics: The Psychology of Small Group Behavior.* New York: McGraw-Hill.

Chapter 10.   Managing Conflict

Filley, A. 1991. *Interpersonal Conflict Resolution.* Glenview, Ill.: Scott, Foresman.

Fisher, R. and Ury, W. 1991. *Getting to Yes: Negotiating Agreement Without Giving In.* New York: Viking Press.

Jandt, F. and Gillette, P. 1985. *Win-Win Negotiating: Turning Conflict into Agreement.* New York: Wiley.

Shaw, M. 1981. *Group Dynamics: The Psychology of Small Group Behavior.* New York: McGraw-Hill.

INDEX